NAMED IN STONE AND SKY

NAMED IN STONE AND SKY

AN ARIZONA ANTHOLOGY

Edited by Gregory McNamee

The University of Arizona Press
Tucson & London

The University of Arizona Press
Copyright © 1993 by Gregory McNamee

♾ This book is printed on acid-free, archival-quality paper.
Manufactured in the United States of America

98   97   96   95   94   93   6   5   4   3   2   1

Library of Congress Cataloging-in-Publication Data

Named in stone and sky : an Arizona anthology / edited by
Gregory McNamee.
    p.   cm.
  Includes bibliographical references and index.
  ISBN 0-8165-1278-7 (acid-free paper). —
  ISBN 0-8165-1348-1 (pbk. : acid-free paper)
  1. American literature—Arizona.   2. Arizona—Literary
collections.   1. McNamee, Gregory.
PS571.A6N35   1993   92-24494
810.8'032791—dc20   CIP

British Cataloguing-in-Publication Data
A catalogue record for this book is available from the British
Library.

Publication of this book is made possible in part by a grant from
the Arizona Commission on the Arts through appropriations
from the Arizona State Legislature and grants from the National
Endowment for the Arts.

Whole sight: or all the rest is desolation.

—John Fowles, *Daniel Martin* (1977)

CONTENTS

✢

INTRODUCTION

Begin on the gunsight northern line and follow the alternating series of red sandstone escarpments and dry washes eastward. At the 109th meridian, track straight south across wide mountain ranges, the drainages of swift rivers soon to be impounded, yucca-studded cliffs. Turn west at the 31st parallel, stair-stepping through grasslands, cactus forests, quartz sand, and lava chaos. This line is straight, too, jogging a little here and there, unsteady evidence of a mapmaker's indecision—the real maker of maps, armed not with a theodolite but a gun. Turn north a few degrees west of the 114th parallel, along the one line that acknowledges geomorphology above politics, along the great, cloudy Colorado River, another victim of human artifice. You have bounded 113,909 square miles of some of the most varied landscapes on the planet.

This place has borne many names, most of them lost to time: Ali shonak. Provincia interna. Diné Bikéyah. Pimería Alta. Dixie. For a fleeting moment in a politician's chambers, Gadsdonia. Finally, Arizona.

Within its sheriff's-badge outline lie other lines, borders that conform only to the passing eons of geological time, to the immutable laws of accretion, erosion, metamorphosis. To the north, the massive dry uplift of the Colorado Plateau, dissected by the Colorado River through the 250-mile length of the Grand Canyon. Below it, the mile-high rise of the Mogollon Rim, its black outcroppings of rhyolite and granite giving way to the jumbled Arizona interior, birthplace of a dozen rivers. To the west, the stark, solar Mojave. To the south, other deserts: the lush Sonoran, the grassy Chihuahuan, basin-and-range provinces broken by southeastward-tending mountain islands, shading off into Old Mexico. These are bio-geographical provinces any one of which would take a lifetime to know.

Many men and women have tried to describe this diverse wealth of places. Late in the nineteenth century, C. Hart Merriam studied the San Francisco Peaks north of Flagstaff and concluded that what made Arizona special was its range of elevations, from near sea level at Yuma to the 12,633-foot rise of Mount Humphreys, his object of study. Lifting a page from the German explorer Alexander von Humboldt, who had mapped the South American cordillera as far north as central Mexico, Merriam developed the notion of "life zones," arriving at a formula whereby every thousand-foot rise in elevation corresponded to the biotic changes one would encounter by traveling three hundred miles north of the Mexican border. In Arizona he counted six such life zones: the Hudsonian, represented only by the highest peaks of the San Francisco range, with their lichen-and-tundra associations that echo those of subarctic climes; the Canadian, marked by the vast coniferous forests of ponderosa pine, spruce, and Douglas fir of the high Mogollon Rim; the Transition zone, where stunted piñon and juniper replace the tall trees; the upper Sonoran, with its mesquite forests and grasslands, beginning at about 6,500 feet, and its characteristic saguaro forests that have come, for better or worse, to stand for the whole of Arizona in a thousand advertisements and Western movies; the lower Sonoran, a zone of sun-scorched sand and black volcanic rock; and the unlikely Tropical, attested to by a few inland oases and the lagoons of the lower Colorado. Although Stephen Pyne, a distinguished student of Arizona's natural and human history, has objected to Merriam's classification as "practically a plagiarism of outmoded ideas" that Humboldt applied only to one place, Mount Chimborazo in the Ecuadorian Andes, it at least provides a starting metaphor for understanding Arizona's immense variety of landforms, of plant and animal life, nearly without equal in the contiguous United States.

Other scientists, whether writing for their peers or for a popular audience, have attempted to delimit Arizona's aspects. The plant geographer Forrest Shreve, for one, spent years trying to work out a satisfactory definition of the term *desert*. "It is impossible," he concluded, "to define desert in terms of a single characteristic, just as truly as it is impossible to differentiate species by such a procedure." He went on to suggest at least a few distinctive features: the irregular and modest rainfall that marks so much of the state; the low level of moisture in all but riparian and alpine soils; the swift winds and correspondingly high evaporation rate of surface waters; the land's poorly developed drainage systems; and rocky or sandy ground.

Three decades later Joseph Wood Krutch, a transplanted Easterner who remains one of Arizona's best-known celebrants, countered, "probably the most satisfactory definition of 'desert' [is] a region where the ground cover is not continuous; where, that is, the earth remains bare of vegetation between such plants as manage to grow." David Quammen, a Faulkner scholar and mystery writer turned naturalist, rejoins, "a desert is one of those entities, like virginity and sans serif typefaces, of which the definition must begin with negatives." And finally, for this is a revisionist age, the architectural historian Reyner Banham urges that what we have before us is not, in the strictest sense, a desert at all—a desolation, that is, a place devoid of people, of life.

Like one trying to capture the whole of the Grand Canyon in the frame of an Instamatic camera, no single authority has yet managed to express the essence of the desert—the essence of so much of Arizona—in words. In his novel *Dalva*, Jim Harrison, a frequent sojourner in these parts, gets at the heart of the matter:

> When you first come to the desert . . . it's just a desert, an accretion of all the bits and pieces of information and opinion you've picked up along the way about deserts. Then you study and walk and camp in the desert for years . . . and it becomes . . . heraldic, mysterious, stupefying, full of auras and ghosts, with the voices of those who lived there speaking from every petroglyph and pottery shard. At this point you must let the desert go back to being the desert or you'll gradually become quite blind to it.

With the scientists and novelists have come artists, ethnographers, historians, and poets to carve out their bit of Arizona and bring it to life in a thousand evocations. "I take SPACE to be the central fact to man born in America, from Folsom cave to now," the poet Charles Olson proclaimed. "I spell it large because it comes large here. Large, and without mercy." Olson's axiom is another starting point for understanding the Arizona landscape, the focus of this anthology. Descriptions of the land—from the Navajo night chant to Mary Austin's survey of Arizona's rivers, from Martha Summerhayes's barely disguised horror on first seeing the Western desert to Simon Ortiz's gaze into Canyon de Chelly—take vastness, too, as a primary definition of this seemingly unending land.

The land richly informs the literature of Arizona. It underlies the etiological myths and creation stories and Coyote tales of the Native American peoples, the inventories of the Spanish *conquistadores* and Anglo military surveyors, the shoot-em-up novels of Zane Grey and Louis L'Amour, the natural histories and romances and poems and *romans noirs* that Arizonans produce today. The land is the central fact here, the constant that joins the best writing about Arizona from one generation to the next.

That writing is often celebratory, and for good reason. Anyone who has awaited the coming of the summer rains in the lower Sonoran zone cannot help but share the joy Barbara Kingsolver allows her characters on first seeing a desert monsoon. No one who has traveled the upper reaches of the Blue River will dispute Aldo Leopold's contention that it behooves us all to learn to "think like a mountain," to recognize and cherish the magic of the uplands. The literature of Arizona is often marked by a sort of primal awe, a reverence for place that will resonate long after our current mania for bulldozers and regional shopping centers has vanished in the ruins of postindustrial civilization.

Occasionally Arizona's chroniclers have afforded us less than celebratory views of the place. (Thankfully, most of them went elsewhere.) At the close of the Mexican-American War, William Tecumseh Sherman, then a captain, surveyed the newly conquered lands of the Southwest. On his return to Washington, President Zachary Taylor asked Sherman, "Will our new possessions pay for the blood and treasure spent in the war?" Sherman replied, "General, I feel we'll have to go to war again." Taylor asked him why. "To make 'em take the damn country back," he said. Maxwell Perkins, the legendary editor who helped launch the careers of F. Scott Fitzgerald, Ernest Hemingway, and Thomas Wolfe, felt much the same way. Writing to the English novelist John Galsworthy, who, having completed seven installments of his epic *Forsyte Saga*, was vacationing near Phoenix, Perkins remarked, "I have very pleasant memories of Arizona, the only flaw I found in it was that any given point in the landscape always looked so much better than it was when you got to it."

Still other writers combine a range of emotions—Edward Abbey, for one, who nearly met his end on a dozen solo journeys up mountains, down canyons, and across vast sweeps of desert. His account in *Desert Solitaire* of one such mission is full of fear, love, humor, anxiety, and tranquility, mixed reactions that Arizona's landscapes can instantaneously inspire. John Gregory Bourke, who traveled over much of Arizona as an officer in the Apache wars, expresses the problem well:

> Dante Alighieri, it has always seemed to me, made the mistake of his life in dying when he did in the picturesque capital of the Exarchate five hundred and fifty years ago. Had he held on to this mortal coil until after Uncle Sam had perfected the "Gadsden Purchase," he would have found full scope for his genius in the description of a region in which not only purgatory and hell, but heaven likewise, had

combined to produce a bewildering kaleidoscope of all that was wonderful, weird, terrible, and awe-inspiring, with not a little that was beautiful and romantic.

This collection gathers representative writings on the widely various landscapes of Arizona, a literature ranging across hundreds of miles and thousands of years. In setting boundaries for the book, I have borrowed Hippocrates's useful observation that a region is made up of not only the places it comprises but also its waters and airs: its sun, lightning, and stars; its rivers, springs, and lakes. Hippocrates's inclusiveness allows us to see a place in its totality, as our contemporary ecologists now urge. I have also appropriated Ezra Pound's notion that "literature is news that stays news"—a comfortably broad definition that endorses, or so it seems to me, the inclusion of newspaper editorials alongside creation stories, of geological reports next to lyric poems, of fictional dialogue against sober historical accounts. The genres necessary to describe them are, happily, as various as the landscape, as the airs, waters, and places that make up Arizona.

In proposing an ideal literature for his native Ireland, William Butler Yeats remarked, "I would have our writers and craftsmen master their history and their legends and fix upon their memory the appearance of mountains and rivers and make it all visible again in their arts." The literature of Arizona, from the songs of the first people to those of its latter-day arrivals, has never been without that kind of memory. What remains is to take that body of writing and speaking and singing as one of many talismans in protecting an Arizona long under siege, to draw on it to free its dammed waters and rescue its plundered forests, to set aside mountaintops and watersheds and deserts for sciences and technologies more humane than the ones we have now. I hope that this little reader proves useful to that end.

GREGORY MCNAMEE

✦ AIRS ✦

HOUSE MADE OF THE DAWN

*The Navajo Night Chant is sung in a complex, nine-day healing ceremony.
Washington Matthews's rendering introduced the chant to Anglo readers in
1902, and it has since become the best-known work of Navajo literature in
English translation. As an evocation of the landscape of the Colorado
Plateau and of Arizona's skies, it is without peer.*

In Tse'gihi
In the house made of the dawn,
In the house made of the evening twilight,
In the house made of the dark cloud,
In the house made of the he-rain,
In the house made of the dark mist,
In the house made of the she-rain,
In the house made of pollen,
In the house made of grasshoppers,
Where the dark mist curtains the doorway,
The path to which is on the rainbow,
Where the zigzag lightning stands high on top,
Where the he-rain stands high on top,
Oh, male divinity!
With your moccasins of dark cloud, come to us.
With your leggings of dark cloud, come to us.
With your shirt of dark cloud, come to us.
With your head-dress of dark cloud, come to us.
With your mind enveloped in dark cloud, come to us.
With the dark thunder above you, come to us soaring.
With the shapen cloud at your feet, come to us soaring.
With the far darkness made of the dark cloud over your head, come to
    us soaring.
With the far darkness made of the he-rain over your head, come to us
    soaring.
With the far darkness made of the dark mist over your head, come to us
    soaring.

With the far darkness made of the she-rain over your head, come to us
soaring.
With the zigzag lightning flung out on high over your head, come to us
soaring.
With the rainbow hanging high over your head, come to us soaring.
With the far darkness made of the dark cloud on the ends of your
wings, come to us soaring.
With the far darkness made of the he-rain on the ends of your wings,
come to us soaring.
With the far darkness made of the dark mist on the ends of your wings,
come to us soaring.
With the far darkness made of the she-rain on the ends of your wings,
come to us soaring.
With the zigzag lightning flung out on high on the ends of your wings,
come to us soaring.
With the rainbow hanging high on the ends of your wings, come to us
soaring.
With the near darkness made of the dark cloud, of the he-rain, of the
dark mist and of the she-rain, come to us.
With the darkness on the earth, come to us.
With these I wish the foam floating on the flowing water over the roots
of the great corn.
I have made your sacrifice.
I have prepared a smoke for you.
My feet restore for me.
My limbs restore for me.
My body restore for me.
My mind restore for me.
My voice restore for me.
To-day, take out your spell for me.
To-day, take away your spell for me.
Away from me you have taken it.
Far off from me it is taken.
Far off you have done it.
Happily I recover.
Happily my interior becomes cool.
Happily my eyes regain their power.
Happily my head becomes cool.
Happily my limbs regain their power.

Happily I hear again.
Happily for me (the spell) is taken off.
Happily I walk (or, may I walk).
Impervious to pain, I walk.
Feeling light within, I walk.
With lively feelings, I walk.
Happily (or in beauty) abundant dark clouds I desire.
Happily abundant dark mists I desire.
Happily abundant passing showers I desire.
Happily an abundance of vegetation I desire.
Happily an abundance of pollen I desire.
Happily abundant dew I desire.
Happily may fair white corn, to the ends of the earth, come with you.
Happily may fair yellow corn, to the ends of the earth, come with you.
Happily may fair blue corn, to the ends of the earth, come with you.
Happily may fair corn of all kinds, to the ends of the earth, come with
    you.
Happily may fair plants of all kinds, to the ends of the earth, come with
    you.
Happily may fair goods of all kinds, to the ends of the earth, come with
    you.
Happily may fair jewels of all kinds, to the ends of the earth, come with
    you.
With these before you, happily may they come with you.
With these behind you, happily may they come with you.
With these below you, happily may they come with you.
With these above you, happily may they come with you.
With these all around you, happily may they come with you.
Thus happily you accomplish your tasks.
Happily the old men will regard you.
Happily the old women will regard you.
Happily the young men will regard you.
Happily the young women will regard you.
Happily the boys will regard you.
Happily the girls will regard you.
Happily the children will regard you.
Happily the chiefs will regard you.
Happily, as they scatter in different directions, they will regard you.
Happily, as they approach their homes, they will regard you.

Happily may their roads home be on the trail of pollen (peace).
Happily may they all get back.
In beauty (happily) I walk.
With beauty before me, I walk.
With beauty behind me, I walk.
With beauty below me, I walk.
With beauty above me, I walk.
With beauty all around me, I walk.
It is finished (again) in beauty,
It is finished in beauty,
It is finished in beauty,
It is finished in beauty.

SONGS FOR THE SUN

Frank Waters recorded this traditional Hopi song of creation in his Book of the Hopi. *Anyone who has seen a sunrise from the Hopi Mesas, a hundred-mile view in any direction, will at once apprehend the singers' delight at the rising morning star.*

The dark purple light rises in the north,
A yellow light rises in the east.
Then we of the flowers of the earth come forth
To receive a long life of joy.
We call ourselves the Butterfly Maidens.

Both male and female make their prayers to the east,
Make the respectful sign to the Sun our Creator.
The sounds of bells ring through the air,
Making a joyful sound throughout the land,
Their joyful echo resounding everywhere.

Humbly I ask my Father,
The perfect one, Taiowa, our Father,
The perfect one creating the beautiful life
Shown to us by the yellow light,
To give us perfect light at the time of the red light.

The perfect one laid out the perfect plan
And gave to us a long span of life,
Creating song to implant joy in life.
On this path of happiness, we the Butterfly Maidens
Carry out his wishes by greeting our Father Sun.

The song resounds back from our Creator with joy.
And we of the earth repeat it to our Creator.
At the appearing of the yellow light,
Repeats and repeats again the joyful echo,
Sounds and resounds for times to come.

✢

The Yaqui are relative newcomers to Arizona, having arrived in number only in the early years of the twentieth century, following a campaign of genocide against them in their native Mexico. Felipe Molina, a Yaqui deer singer and poet, sings this composition about the growing flower, a beautiful kenning for the sun. The seyewailo *is the enchanted flower world that, in the Yaqui worldview, exists parallel to our own.*

———————————

Growing flower, growing flower,
Flower went with the enchanted dawn wind.
With the dawn wind's air you are flying,
With the enchanted, enchanted dawn wind you went.

Over yonder, on the side of the *seyewailo,*
On the top of the enchanted world,
You fly so high.
Beautifully, endlessly, you go sparkling.
You went with the enchanted dawn wind.

THE CLIMATE OF SONORA

Ignaz Pfefferkorn (1725–1793) spent seven years in Sonora, a province of New Spain that included southern Arizona, as a Jesuit priest among the Eudeve, Opata, and Tohono O'odham peoples. The ruins of the church built for him by the last group may still be seen at Guevavi, near present-day Nogales. Expelled from New Spain with the Jesuit order in 1767, Pfefferkorn returned to his native Germany, where he wrote Beschreibung der Landschaft Sonora, *translated by Theodore Treutlein as* Sonora: A Description of the Province, *from which this passage is taken.*

Although Sonora is situated outside the torrid zone, beginning in the twenty-seventh degree of north latitude, it is nevertheless, on the whole, a very warm country. By February one is bothered by the sun, though the heat is not continual in this month. For one or two days it is almost as warm as Germany in the hot summer-time, but immediately thereafter it is cold again. On a given day the weather may be so changeable that one feels great heat and severe cold, and not infrequently this change takes place in the space of two or three hours. The reason for this change is the inconstancy of the winds, which blow from all points of the compass. In March the heat rises, although this month also is often subject to changes. By May the heat is already as intense as it usually is in Germany toward the end of June. It rises until the end of July and continues so to the end of September. October and thence to about the end of December is really the most comfortable time, this period being comparable to the mild spring months in Germany. The sun is so moderately warm that it is not vexatious, nor does it become cold. Only the morning and evening hours and the nights are cool, though so moderately that a single bedcover provides enough warmth for the night.

Toward the end of December, winter and low temperatures commence. This condition lasts through January to the beginning of February, and is very similar to that which one is accustomed to experience along the Rhine River in March during years of average winter. When north winds blow they cover the fields with frost, but never with snow, and it is considered an astonishing occurrence and a sign of severe cold if snow falls on the plains. In the eleven years which I spent in Sonora, this happened only once, in the year 1761.[1] However, the snow disappeared after it had remained on the ground only a few minutes. It is often seen, indeed, on high mountain peaks, but there also the sun does not allow it to remain for long. Now and then ice forms on the edges of brooks, and thin sheets of it will cover little pools also; but in houses water never freezes. Moreover, the cold is so tolerable that one can well do without having a stove in the room. A German needs nothing more than a good mantle to protect himself sufficiently against the cold, but a Sonora-born Spaniard, on the other hand, who cannot endure any cold, is somewhat more sensitive and must at times take refuge at a fire, which he builds under the open sky. The Indians, who have no clothes or covers . . . tend a small fire throughout the night to warm themselves in their lowly and tightly closed huts.

The summer heat begins in May, as already stated, and lasts until the end of September. One would think that the heat would be greatest in Sonora, as it is here in Germany, in the second half of the summer; however, experience proves the opposite. May, June, and July are noticeably hotter than the months which follow, since no winds blow in those three months, and, if there is a stray breeze, it is so weak that it cannot cool the atmosphere. Besides, as a rule, not a drop of rain falls from the beginning of January to the end of June. Consequently the earth as well as the air is greatly parched by the sun's burning rays, augmented by the so-called *quemazones,* or conflagrations. . . .

Since the heat in May, June, and July is already so intense, it would necessarily be quite unbearable during the hot season in August and September were the heat not moderated, in Sonora as in New Spain in general, by daily rains. Consequently, this season is called *tiempo de aguas,*[2] or the rainy period. It begins in July and ends in September. The rain is not continuous, but passes off in two or three hours. However, the precipitation is so heavy that brooks and rivers are extraordinarily swollen and are very dangerous to those who, because of pressing need or audacity, would cross them on horseback, for there are no bridges in this country. When the storm has ended, the rivers fall again as rapidly as they

1. In 1761, Pfefferkorn was attached to the mission at Atí, today's Atil, lying at an elevation of 1,200 feet in the Altar Valley south of Sasabe.
2. The Spanish phrase is still used in Arizona. The English equivalent, introduced perhaps ironically, is "the monsoon season."

have risen, and the sky assumes its former brightness. These rain showers are not general; at times they affect a stretch of but a few miles, over which the rain-cloud empties itself, while the surrounding regions remain completely dry. Where rain does not occur for some days, field products, especially maize or Indian corn, stand in danger of drying up, because it is not everywhere possible to irrigate the country from ditches. However, such a misfortune is not very often to be feared. After the first heavy shower the heat is indescribable, so that at night as well as in the day-time one nearly suffocates. After some days, though, the air becomes cooled by repeated rains and the heat so moderated that it is quite bearable.

Sonora, through these daily rains, receives a pleasant relief from the heat, and at the same time its products are increased. Hence, these rains would surely be considered as priceless blessings of nature were they not always accompanied by the most horrible thunder-storms, which not infrequently do great damage to men and animals in the villages and in the fields. One cannot listen to the continuous crashing of the thunder without shuddering. At times such thunder-storms bring with them a damaging hail, which destroys all growing things in the field and garden; or there may occur a ruinous cloudburst, in Sonora called *culebra de agua*, or water snake,[3] which will flood over country and villages, devastating them. Sometimes the thunder-storms are accompanied by violent wind-storms and whirlwinds, which lift the sand in a very thick, twisted column almost to the clouds. Nothing these whirlwinds seize can withstand their power. Even the strongest trees are often uprooted, roofs are uncovered, and houses upset, if they are not very solid. It is noteworthy that these thunder-storms and heavy showers never occur in the morning but always in the afternoon. Mornings the sky is entirely clear, but afternoons clouds form and two or three hours thereafter there breaks out the fearful thunder-storm, which sometimes returns at night and rages again. Hence, during these months everyone avoids traveling in the afternoon if possible, because of the constant danger of being caught in such a storm. Therefore, wherever one reaches a shelter around noon, or even a little before, the day's journey is ended.

This three-month rainy season ends, indeed, as has already been stated,

---

3. Folklorist James Griffith identifies this association between water and snakes as a manifestation of the Uto-Aztecan Water Serpent motif, variants of which have been found as far north as the Hopi Mesas and as far south as Panama. An elderly vaquero described the devastating flood of October 1983 to Griffith as *una media culebra* (half a snake).

in September. However, this is true only of the daily showers accompanied by terrific thunder-storms, for quiet, gentle rains occur intermittently in the three months following. These are general rains which last from one to three days. It even happens, although very seldom, that they continue eight, nine, or ten days. Twice in eleven years I experienced this; the one time it rained ten, the other twelve days and nights, practically without ceasing. At this time the rivers rose over their banks, flooded the surrounding regions, made the roads impassable, and cut off communications with the neighboring villages. Even in the houses, one was afforded little protection. In Sonora the roofs are in very poor condition, since they consist only of twigs with earth thrown upon them. When the water has penetrated them, they drip continuously. Consequently, in such a protracted rain there remained hardly a spot where one could find shelter.

SUMMER SKIES

From 1898 to 1901, John Van Dyke, a courtly Easterner, roamed the deserts of California, Arizona, and Sonora on horseback, a fox terrier his customary and often sole company. Van Dyke took his fortunes as they came, dining some evenings on hardtack and alkali-laden water under a solitary mesquite tree, others on fine beef and wines in well-appointed ranch houses. Wherever he went, he found reason to celebrate the arid places he visited.

He had seemingly few of the makings of a desert rat. An art historian and professor of aesthetics at Rutgers University, Van Dyke (1856–1932) was interested in the qualities of light in landscapes and in how those qualities could be translated into painting. The book that he made of his travels in this country, The Desert, *is in fact subtitled "Further Studies in Natural Appearances," and it contains many acute observations on the play of light on the mountains, the sand, and the sky. Bibliographer Lawrence Clark Powell has noted, with good cause, that* The Desert *is the book from which the modern literature of the Southwest has grown.*

In the following passage, Van Dyke is somewhere west of Tucson, near the Baboquivari Mountains. He often traveled without maps and was seldom absolutely sure of his whereabouts—perhaps the best way to see the desert after all.

I ride away through the thin mesquite and the little adobe ranch house is soon lost to view. The morning is still and perfectly clear. The stars have gone out, and the moon is looking pale, the deep blue is warming, the sky is lightening with the coming day. How cool and crystalline the air! In a few hours the great plain will be almost like a fiery furnace under the rays of the summer sun, but now it is chilly. And in a few hours there will be rings and bands and scarves of heat set wavering across the waste upon the opalescent wings of the mirage; but now the air is so clear that one can see the breaks in the rocky face of the mountain range, though it is fully twenty miles away. It may be further. Who of the desert has not spent his day riding at a mountain and never even reaching its base? This is a land of illusions and thin air. The vision is so cleared at times that the truth itself is deceptive. But I shall ride on for several hours. If, by twelve o'clock, the foot hills are not reached, I shall turn back.

The summer heat has withered everything except the mesquite, the palo verde, the grease wood, and the various cacti. Under foot there is a little dry grass, but more often patches of bare gravel and sand rolled in shallow beds that course toward the large valleys. In the draws and flat places the fine sand lies thicker, is tossed in wave forms by the wind, and banked high against clumps of cholla or prickly pear. In the wash-outs and over the cut banks of the arroyos it is sometimes heaped in mounds and crests like driven snow. It blows here along the boundary line between Arizona and Sonora almost every day; and the tailing of the sands behind the bushes shows that the prevailing winds are from the Gulf region. A cool wind? Yes, but only by comparison with the north wind. When you feel it on your face you may think it the breath of some distant volcano.

How pale-blue the Lost Mountains look under the growing light. I am watching their edges develop into broken barriers of rock, and even as I watch the tallest tower of all is struck with a bright fawn color. It is the high point to catch the first shaft of the sun. Quickly the light spreads downward until the whole ridge is tinged by it, and the abrupt sides of porphyry begin to glow under it. It is not long before great shafts of light alternating with shadow stretch down the plain ahead of me. The sun is streaming through the tops of the eastern mountains and the sharp pointed pinnacles are cutting shadows in the broad beam of light.

That beam of light! Was there ever anything so beautiful! How it flashes its color through shadow, how it gilds the tops of the mountains and gleams white on the dunes of the desert! In any land what is there more glorious than sunlight! Even here in the desert, where it falls fierce and hot as a rain of meteors, it is the one supreme beauty to which all things pay allegiance. The beast and the bird are not too fond of its heat and as soon as the sun is high in the heavens they seek cover in the canyons; but for all that the chief glory of the desert is its broad blaze of omnipresent light.

In Richard Hinton's Hand-Book to Arizona, *an unnamed government surveyor, posted to the middle Colorado in the 1870s and moved by less exalted visions than Van Dyke's, describes the withering summer climate of Fort Mojave and environs. The area, in northwestern Arizona, continues to boast the state's consistently highest temperatures.*

From the middle of June to the 1st of October panting humanity finds no relief from the heat. As soon as the sun appears above the horizon its heat is felt, and this continues to increase until a maximum is reached about three o'clock in the afternoon, after which the temperature falls slowly, and oftentimes very slowly, until sunrise. During the hottest part of the day exertion of any kind is impossible; even while lying perfectly quiet the perspiration oozes from the skin and runs from the body in numerous streams. Everything feels hot to the touch, and metallic objects cannot be handled without producing blisters upon the skin. The white sand reflects the heat and blinds the traveller by its glare. Rain scarcely ever falls during the summer months, and not more than three or four inches of rain the year round. The atmosphere is so dry and evaporation so rapid that the water in our canteens, if the cover was kept moist, kept a temperature of 30 deg. below that of the air. Great quantities of water are drunk during these hot days, and no uncomfortable fullness is experienced. One gallon per man, and sometimes two, was the daily consumption. Notwithstanding the excessive heat, no sunstrokes occurred, although we were at one time exposed in a narrow cañon to a temperature of 120 deg. All of the party preserved good health during the summer. There is no danger of catching cold in this climate, even if wet to the skin three or four times during the day or night. No dew or moisture is deposited during the night, hence no covering is required. The hot wind which blows frequently from the south is the most disagreeable feature of the climate. No matter where you go, it is sure to find you out and give you the full benefit of a gust that feels as if it issued from a blast-furnace, and parches the skin and tongue in an instant. Then there is no recourse but to take copious draughts from the canteens to keep up the supply of moisture in the body. If water cannot be obtained, the delirium of thirst soon overpowers the unfortunate traveller, and he dies a horrible death.

The landscape of the soul often reflects that of one's place, as this lyric by Nancy Mairs, "In the Dry Season," demonstrates.

Here
is need
for the forgiveness of rain.

Green greyed
by dust and the white sear of sun
flesh shrivels
ground cracked at the root.

Here
the dry vigil

of the snake
milk-eyed
within the shadow of stone

of the seed split

the wait
for the rustle in brittlebush
in mesquite
for the fragrance of stirred dust

signifying rain.

Bless me:
I have thorns.

Bless me:
I have bitter water
at my heart.

*Ross Calvin (1889–1970) moved to Silver City, New Mexico, in 1927,
where he took up office as the town's Episcopalian priest. Seven years later
he published his reflections on his newfound homeland in* Sky Determines:
An Interpretation of the Southwest. *In the 1940s he traveled the length of the
Gila River from its source in the Mogollon Mountains near Silver City to its*

confluence with the Colorado above Yuma, a journey that he recorded in
River of the Sun (1946). Here, with an attention to color and appearance
that John Van Dyke would surely have admired, Calvin describes his first
glimpse of the Sierra Estrella, south of Phoenix.

Most notable of all in the desert is the glory which resides in its light and
color. In the more restricted sense of the word it is ethereal, because it
inheres not in actual cliff and canyon but is added by the ether through
which things are viewed. The fantastic mountains painted by Maxfield
Parrish are not drawn from imagination; they are drawn from Arizona.
There the most commonplace dawn has its eerie, unearthly lighting.

When the sun is low, its beams aflame with color, then the Superstitions, to name but one group, are a cobalt spectacle for which language is
totally incompetent. That holds, too, for the Maricopas, the Mohawks,
and dozens of the other strictly desert ranges. But none can surpass the
Sierra Estrella, of the queenly appellation meaning Mountain of the Star,
as she rises air-blue with distance against the orange sunset.

All who have ever tried to describe desert mountains, and all who have
ever painted them have failed to record and fix the charm that for me is the
final one. I mean their curious absence of identity with aught of earth or
sky. Sierra Estrella is obviously not a violet cloud on the horizon, for there
is no such authentic, substantial violet in the sky. And it is equally lacking
in identity with anything about the prosaic Phoenix plain which stretches
from my eye to the line where her feet seem to rest. Earthy mesquite brush
can have nothing in common with that pure color.

Sierra Estrella viewed at a distance of ten leagues or so belongs neither
to plain nor to sky but is a lovely blue apparition of the air. Yet blue is
inadequate, for there are hours when she is red—as red as roses would be
were they visible thirty miles. But in her most regal moments, she is of the
hue of irises, the firmament above her at first pure yellow, then deepening
in sequence to orange and fiery crimson, as night seems to overtake the
flying sun. No forested peak can ever equal her coloration, for green
slopes in any light are green, more or less; while stone pinnacles and cliffs
of lilac or garnet, dyed by the evening light, will take on tints of delicacy
and splendor beside which green is homespun. Sierra Estrella, lady of the
star, clad in dawn or sunset, I salute you!

❖

Yuma, the site of the Arizona Territorial Prison and the Colorado River crossing at the end of the Camino del Diablo, inspired little admiration in early travelers who saw it in summertime. With customary embellishment, J. Ross Browne (1821–1875), who toured Arizona in the early 1860s, describes the airs of Yuma in winter and summer in this passage from his Adventures in the Apache Country. *His tale of the soldier (variously the prospector and the cowboy) and the blanket has passed into Arizona folklore.*

_____

The climate in winter is finer than that of Italy. It would scarcely be possible to suggest an improvement. I never experienced such exquisite Christmas weather as we enjoyed during our sojourn. Perhaps fastidious people might object to the temperature in summer, when the rays of sun attain their maximum force, and the hot winds sweep in from the desert. It is said that a wicked soldier died here, and was consigned to the fiery regions below for his manifold sins; but unable to stand the rigors of the climate, sent for his blankets. I have even heard the complaint made that the thermometer failed to show the true heat because the mercury dried up. Every thing dries; wagons dry; men dry; chickens dry; there is no juice left in any thing, living or dead, by the close of summer. Officers and soldiers are supposed to walk about creaking; mules, it is said, can only bray at midnight; and I have heard it hinted that the carcasses of cattle rattle inside their hides, and that snakes find a difficulty in bending their bodies, and horned frogs die of apoplexy. Chickens hatched at this season, as old Fort Yumers say, come out of the shell ready cooked; bacon is eaten with a spoon. . . . The Indians sit in the river with fresh mud on their heads, and by dint of constant dipping and sprinkling manage to keep from roasting, though they usually come out parboiled.

With the advent of air-conditioning, Yuma has grown into Arizona's third-largest city. An uncooled summer there, however, would today doubtless produce a poem much like Charles Phelps's ode "Yuma," first published in

1882. Phelps's simoon, derived from the Arabic term samúm (poison), is a violent, sand- or dust-laden wind common to the deserts of the world.

Weary, weary, desolate,
Sand-swept, parched, and cursed of fate;
Burning, but how passionless!
Barren, bald, and pitiless!

Through all ages baleful moons
Glared upon thy whited dunes;

And malignant, wrathful suns
Fiercely drank thy streamless runs;

So that Nature's only tune
Is the blare of the simoon
Piercing burnt unweeping skies
With its awful monodies.

Not a flower lifts its head
Where the emigrant lies dead;

Not a living creature calls
Where the Gila Monster crawls
Hot and hideous as the sun
To the dead man's skeleton;

But the desert and the dead,
And the hot hell overhead,
And the blazing, seething air,
And the dead mirage are there.

In The Colorado *Frank Waters remembers mountainous Bisbee as a place "where postmen don't deliver letters to the door; the wooden stairs are too high and steep." Lawrence Ferlinghetti, a leading Beat Generation poet, has often read his work at the Bisbee Poetry Festival, an annual event that in*

recent years has contributed to the southeastern Arizona mining town's rebirth as an artistic center. These stanzas from Ferlinghetti's "Mule Mountain Dreams" capture the feel of a desert summer evening.

White hot sun fallen
   over the stone rim
      of the steep hills
         of Bisbee, Arizona

the tops of the hills still aglow
   in white sunlight
      the air still bright above them

the little weather-beat hillside houses
   still incandescent
      with leftover sun
         fade like filaments
            in turned-off light-bulbs

and await
   the desert mountain night
      windows agape like mouths
         to breathe the first
            cool night air

In my memory somewhere
a donkey brays
No border exists
The Mexican night
            closes in

NAMING LIGHTNING

The assignment of names to events in nature and to the land lies at the foundation of storytelling, from the ancient Irish dindsenchas *to the Australian aboriginal naming-walks that Bruce Chatwin describes in* The Songlines. *Native American literature abounds with examples of imaginative naming, as in this Quechan (Yuma) origin myth that storyteller Charles Wilson told to anthropologist A. M. Halpern in 1938. The story was subsequently published in* Spirit Mountain: An Anthology of Yuman Story and Song, *edited by Leanne Hinton and Lucille J. Watahomigie.*

That thing that you call "lightning" is nothing else but a cloud that is white.

The one who is there started there and descended. Wonder Boy—he carries nothing but a bow, and he has one unfeathered arrow to go with it. Standing there he said, "It is I whose lightning it is."

Having descended, he says, "I will go throughout the length of this earth describing things." He said that it was a song. "I will name it, and people will call it 'lightning.'" . . .

That land belongs to him, he says, "Fog Bearer" [San Jacinto Peak, near Yuma]," and he went off describing it. He arrived there and saw it; it stood there as a high white mass; he is on its summit dancing and so he describes it. . . .

Ball of cloud

That cloud comes from the west in the form of a ball of vapor, and he sees it and stands describing it.

He sees the ball of cloud

"I will describe it," he says, and describing it he stands there speaking.

He describes the ball of cloud

He stands describing the same cloud. The clouds came along and stayed in the middle of the sky passing in and out amongst one another. "Well, I will describe it," he said and stood there singing.

Spotty clouds moving about
Clouds going

Clouds in the distance
He describes the distant clouds

The so-called "foggy cloud" drops and falls on his body, and he feels it as he goes along. "I will describe you, you are fog," he says, and stands describing it.

He sees the quivering foggy cloud
He describes the quivering foggy cloud
He sees the cloud passing
He describes the cloud passing
He is looking at the clouds as they turn this way and that
He describes the clouds turning this way and that

"In a similar way I will describe the same cloud," he says. Glancing toward the heavens, he saw the cloud in the form of narrow strips that were almost joined together. It was there that he wanted to be, so he stood describing it.

Cloud strips are there
He describes the cloud strips
Colored clouds are there
He describes the colored clouds

The same cloud being placed in the west, it became pitch dark there, and lightning was placed there and brought straight down from there, so that lightning should flash. He saw it happening and stood describing it.

He sees lightning
Lightning flashes in the darkness
He describes lightning

The desert is a fragile environment, and the people living in it are necessarily fragile as well, much as swimming pools and air conditioners might make us think otherwise. The images in Richard Elman's poem "Cool Lightning Over Tucson" capture both vulnerabilities.

Inside this broken bulb
shards stand up as mountains
and every so often a filament
in the night glows jaggedly,
as though a fingernail ripped
apart the ozone-laden sky.
Thunder beyond the Catalinas
rocks the interstates, plunders
the long bare desert silence.
The broken bulb we live in
glows and then fades and glows
again: night is a soft powder
of iron filings shaken down
upon the saguaros.

SONGS TO PULL DOWN THE CLOUDS

Every June the Tohono O'odham, or Desert People, gather to drink wine made from the fruit of the saguaro cactus, thereby encouraging the arrival of rain. An important element in this act is a repeated invocation for the clouds to appear, and with them the blessing of the water they bear. Tohono O'odham scholar and poet Ofelia Zepeda offers this translation.

And somewhere along the way I stopped again
And it was my cloud that reached me
And it was sprinkling wetly
And here I reached your rainhouse and looked in
There lay many winds, there lay many clouds,
    there lay many seeded things
And you set them down and sat upon them
And with them I touched you
And you moved and breathed your wind
And with it were doing things
Here you dropped it upon my land
And with that my land was sprinkled
    with water and was finished.

The noted anthropologist Ruth Underhill recorded a number of rain songs as they were sung by Tohono O'odham elders in the 1930s. The rain ceremony is described both in her hallmark study Singing for Power *and, five decades later, in Gary Paul Nabhan's* The Desert Smells Like Rain.

The sun is setting,
The mountain shadow

Covers me and stretches on.
In front of the great mountain
Darkness comes forth
And speedily it moves.

  •   •   •

The sun children
Are running westward
Hand in hand,
Madly singing,
Running.

  •   •   •

Where stands the cloud, trembling
On Quijotoa Mountain,
The cloud trembling,
There lies my heart
Trembling.

  •   •   •

Within Quijotoa Mountain
There is thunder.
I looked through it and saw
In every direction
Light!

  •   •   •

Wind came, clouds came.
I sat above them.
Underneath, the mirage glittered.
Rain fell,
The mirage was gone.

  •   •   •

Upon the Children's Land
The waters run and overflow,
Upon the Stream-bed Mountain
The waters run and overflow.

•   •   •

At the edge of the world
It is growing light.
Up rears the light.
Just yonder the day dawns,
Spreading over the night.

> *The Akimel O'odham—the River People, or Pima, cousins to the Tohono O'odham—have a saying: "The rain is blind and must be led by a sandstorm."*

> *The Navajo recognize two kinds of rain, male and female, so named for obvious reasons. Poet Agnes Tso explains their differences.*

MALE RAIN

He comes
   riding on the wind
      kicking up dust
         bending the trees
            blowing flakes of rain
He flees past my window
   to a distant rumble

In-laws beware of him
who mocks the braves
as his features are majestic illusions
his knife the cutting cold
and his soul a drifter

FEMALE RAIN

she pregnant with rain child
comes
> quite
>> softly
>>> and gently
in the night

At dawn she gives birth
> to little droplets of rain
>> and for days on end

AWAKENING

male rain has come and gone
female rain is fading in the distance
father sun is here
and mother earth is awakening

*Whenever it appears in Arizona, rain is a blessing, as poet E. A. Brininstool,
best known for his scholarly biography of Crazy Horse, proclaims in "The
Coming of the Rain" (1914). He wears his Robert Burns influence proudly,
but "dull-eyed herds of cattle" is pure Tennyson.*

There's a whisper on the mesa,
> There's a murmur on the hills,
And the dusty, dry arroyo
> With a new life throbs and thrills.
Where the range was bare and lifeless,
> And the sun-glare scorched the plain,
Lo, the brown earth is rejoicing
> At the coming of the rain!

The sickly grass is turning
> From the sodden brown to green,

With the dusty stain of summer
  Disappearing in between.
From its long, unbroken slumber
  It is waking once again,
With a song of joy and gladness
  At the coming of the rain.

And the dull-eyed herds of cattle
  Low their pleasure at the change
Which transforms the lifeless mesas
  Into miles of greening range.
Soon the blooms will smile a welcome,
  And in grandeur they will reign,
And the soft breeze croon a joy-song
  At the coming of the rain.

The yucca plumes will glisten
  Far upon the mountain height—
Hoary sentinels on duty
  In their gleaming caps of white.
And the cactus and the greasewood
  Will be washing off its stain,
And be clothed in greening garments
  At the coming of the rain.

Down along the rocky ridges
  Will the rain-song sing its way;
It will drip and patter softly
  O'er the sagebrush seas of gray;
And the whole wide range so barren,
  With a glory new will reign,
And all Nature voice its rapture
  At the coming of the rain.

MONSOON

Barbara Kingsolver's first novel, The Bean Trees, *was published to critical acclaim in 1988. It centers on a young woman, Taylor Greer, who leaves a hardscrabble life in rural Kentucky and goes west in a battered 1955 Volkswagen. On the road she falls into the custody of an infant American Indian girl named Turtle. The two eventually arrive in Tucson, where they find a home among Central American refugees at a roadside used-tire store and become involved in the sanctuary movement.*

Here Kingsolver, who has published a study of the Clifton-Morenci copper strike of the early 1980s and several other books, describes a Sonoran Desert thunderstorm as witnessed by her newcomer narrator. Taylor echoes T. E. Lawrence's remark that the desert is, above all, clean.

The whole Tucson Valley lay in front of us, resting in its cradle of mountains. The sloped desert plain that lay between us and the city was like a palm stretched out for a fortuneteller to read, with its mounds and hillocks, its life lines and heart lines of dry stream beds.

A storm was coming up from the south, moving slowly. It looked something like a huge blue-gray shower curtain being drawn along by the hand of God. You could just barely see through it, enough to make out the silhouette of the mountains on the other side. From time to time nervous white ribbons of lightning jumped between the mountaintops and the clouds. A cool breeze came up behind us, sending shivers along the spines of the mesquite trees.

The birds were excited, flitting along the ground and perching on thin, wildly waving weed stalks.

What still amazed me about the desert was all the life it had in it. Hillbilly that I was, I had come to Arizona expecting an endless sea of sand dunes. I'd learned of deserts from old Westerns and Quickdraw McGraw cartoons. But this desert was nothing like that. There were bushes and trees and weeds here, exactly the same as anywhere else, except that the colors were different, and everything alive had thorns.

Mattie told us the names of things, but the foreign words rolled right back out of my ears. I only remembered a few. The saguaros were the great big spiny ones, as tall as normal trees but so skinny and personlike that you always had the feeling they were looking over your shoulder. Around their heads, at this time of year, they wore crowns of bright red fruits split open like mouths. And the ocotillos were the dead-looking thorny sticks that stuck up out of the ground in clusters, each one with a flaming orange spike of flower buds at its top. These looked to me like candles from hell.

Mattie said all the things that looked dead were just dormant. As soon as the rains came they would sprout leaves and grow. It happened so fast, she said, you could practically watch it.

As the storm moved closer it broke into hundreds of pieces so that the rain fell here and there from the high clouds in long, curving gray plumes. It looked like maybe fifty or sixty fires scattered over the city, except that the tall, smoky columns were flowing in reverse. And if you looked closely you could see that in some places the rain didn't make it all the way to the ground. Three-quarters of the way down from the sky it just vanished into the dry air.

Rays of sunlight streamed from between the clouds, like the Holy Ghost on the cover of one of Mattie's dead husband's magazines. Lightning hit somewhere nearby and the thunder made Esperanza and me jump. It wasn't all that close, really, about two miles according to Mattie. She counted the seconds between the lightning strike and the thunder. Five seconds equaled one mile, she told us.

One of the plumes of rain was moving toward us. We could see big drops spattering on the ground, and when it came closer we could hear them, as loud as pebbles on a window. Coming fast. One minute we were dry, then we were being pelted with cold raindrops, then our wet shirts were clinging to our shoulders and the rain was already on the other side of us. All four of us were jumping and gasping because of the way the sudden cold took our breath away. Mattie was counting out loud between the lightning and thunderclaps: six, seven, boom! . . . four, five, six, boom! Estevan danced with Esperanza, then with me, holding his handkerchief under his arm and then twirling it high in the air—it was a flirtatious, marvelous dance with thunder for music. I remembered how he and I had once jumped almost naked into an icy stream together, how long ago that seemed, and how innocent, and now I was madly in love with him, among other people. I couldn't stop laughing. I had never felt so happy.

That was when we smelled the rain. It was so strong it seemed like more than just a smell. When we stretched out our hands we could practically feel it rising up from the ground. I don't know how a person could ever describe that scent. It certainly wasn't sour, but it wasn't sweet either, not like a flower. "Pungent" is the word Estevan used. I would have said "clean." To my mind it was like nothing so much as a wonderfully clean, scrubbed pine floor.

Mattie explained that it was caused by the greasewood bushes, which she said produced a certain chemical when it rained. I asked her if anybody had ever thought to bottle it, it was so wonderful. She said no, but that if you paid attention you could even smell it in town. That you could always tell if it was raining in any part of the city.

I wondered if the smell was really so great, or if it just seemed that way to us. Because of what it meant.

Portal, Arizona, is one of the state's more isolated towns, not by difficulty of terrain but mere remoteness. Tucked on the eastern slope of the Chiricahua Mountains of southeastern Arizona along the New Mexico line, Portal is also one of the lovelier spots in the state—the normally taciturn novelist and lepidopterist Vladimir Nabokov, who spent the summer of 1953 collecting butterflies there, called it "a magnificent place." Journalist and biographer Hank Messick, who has made Portal his home since the 1960s, draws on daily life there for the stuff of the good-natured essays that make up his Desert Sanctuary, *among them this reflection on the effects of rain.*

Across the valley in New Mexico, highway signs advise that Courtesy Pays. At least they do during the dry season. Come July, however, the triangular signs are unfolded and become diamond-shaped. The message then is not to enter the dip ahead if it has water in it.

Arizona, as usual, is more casual, less specific, content to warn the low spot ahead may be a Flash Flood Area. Despite the warnings, a number of people die each year when caught in a dip or culvert by a wave of unexpected water. I thought it strange that most such deaths occur in the larger cities, Phoenix and Tucson, until I drove west one day along Grant [Road] in the middle of a moderate rain storm. Every side street was a roaring river and each intersection a churning lake. Only then did I realize that downtown Tucson has no storm drains, no place for surface water to run. Each year they let God knows how many millions of gallons of water go to waste while the American taxpayer pays billions to bring water across the mountains from the Colorado River. It has something to do with rugged individualism, I suppose.

Trouble can also happen in unpaved areas, as I learned one afternoon while returning from Douglas with a car full of groceries. It had rained hard in Douglas, but for the last thirty miles the sky had been blue, the blacktop dry, so I took State Line Road without a qualm. It bypasses the village of Rodeo and saves perhaps a couple of miles. Since the state line runs up the middle of the road, neither state has seen fit to pave it. Usually it is in good shape, however, and so it seemed today until I began to spot a few puddles and then a lake into which the road entered to exit a couple of hundred feet ahead. Only then did it dawn on me that it had been raining hard here only minutes before, and the runoff from the west was pouring across the road to meet the runoff from the east.

Faye protested rather strongly, but I told her the water couldn't be very deep. There was no real dip along the road, just a few low places. So in we went and in the middle of it the motor stopped.

There we sat with muddy water all around us and no one else within miles. My wife inquired rather caustically what I intended to do. As a man, it was my task to find a solution. I suggested we simply wait where we were. The water would drain off in an hour or two. That met only indignation. I needed no reminder that her arthritis required little excuse to flare up, so I rolled my trouser legs and opened the door. Muddy water gushed in, bringing a scream from my wife who lifted her feet above the torrent and informed me that I was insane. Instead of replying, I stepped into the cold water, after putting the automatic shift into neutral, waded around to the rear, and began to push. I slipped and shuffled a bit but the car was still on a slight down grade and it began to move. Pushing harder still, I tried to gain a little momentum. All the while Faye was steering with one hand, holding her feet above the water with the other, and yelling that I would have a heart attack. I thought she might be right, but I kept on pushing. Just as I was becoming exhausted I realized we were climbing. . . . I moved the little car an additional twenty or thirty feet. It was enough. When I opened the door, some of the water gushed out. The motor started and we made it home without incident. Next day Faye was able to laugh about it.

Such sudden storms were not new to me. In that long summer of house-building, I learned firsthand of the frightful ferocity they embody. Having nothing better to do one August day, I proposed to hike from the top of our property around the shoulder of Portal Peak to the Cathedral Rock Lodge where we were staying. The route led up a deep cove between the mountain and a high foothill to a saddle (pass), after which you walked along deer trails if you could find any to the high place where Martin and Kay Muma were trying to get their rammed-earth house built. A driveway led down from that site, crossed Cave Creek, and went on by the Lodge. A two-hour walk, I estimated in my innocence. A year or two later all of Portal Peak was officially designated a "Wilderness Area," and well it deserves the title.

Faye drove me up to where the cove began and then went home to watch my progress across the side of the mountain through binoculars. I walked along slowly, taking time to explore various pits where dreamers of the past had hoped to strike it rich. All were in the National Forest, and I found pieces of old cars, abandoned drill bits, and some huge hunks of mining machinery as unrusted as the day they were hauled there. Looking back down the cove, I noticed a black cloud to the south, but it didn't worry me. It wasn't until I reached the saddle that I realized the storm was gaining on me.

What to do? To go back would not help; there was no shelter there. Ahead was the rugged, rocky mountainside, cut with deep ravines, and steep. Yet up there was also the end of the trail.

I stepped up the pace, moving as rapidly as the terrain allowed. Abruptly, the awful shadow of the storm was over me. The wind began to blow against my back, and lightning leaped to the ground ahead with a roar that almost knocked me off my feet. Then came the rain, great sheets of it. Within two minutes, the gullies were full of water. I tried to find deer trails, knowing they would cross the most favorable places, but in the growing darkness it became impossible. I was reduced to sliding down one side and crawling up the other.

Lightning sounded again and again, jagged streaks not on a distant horizon but all around me. The rain came harder and harder. I was soaked, my boots full of water. My hat kept blowing off my head. Desperately I looked for an outcropping of rock under which I could take refuge, but there was no place to hide. Of rocks there were plenty, some as large as houses, but they were round or square. Caves existed higher on the mountain, but I wasn't about to climb Portal Peak in search of them.

Despite my discomfort, my alarm at the loose electricity crashing around me, I noted with amazement that the mountain had become a vertical lake. So much water had fallen, it couldn't run off that sleep slope fast enough. I was wading in from two to four inches of water. The ravines were running two feet deep or more. Going down one side I slipped and only a quick grasp at a juniper root kept me from tumbling head first into a deep pool. I was lucky the rock-choked washes were so narrow. Usually I could reach across for tree limbs or other handhold so the force of the water couldn't pull me down. Even so I fell repeatedly. A salty taste in my mouth made me realize I was bleeding somewhere. It proved later to be only a deep scratch across my forehead.

Boom went the lightning. Cold now, and miserable, I struggled on. Through the driving rain I could see the outline of walls. Rammed-earth walls. But I had not maintained my altitude in fighting my way across the shoulder. I'd strike the Mumas' road further down. First, however, I had to get through a forest of mesquite. Holding my arms over my eyes, I drove through, oblivious to the pain. And, thank God, there ahead was the narrow winding road leading down to the Lodge where a hot shower would be my first priority.

I had forgotten the creek. There was no bridge, of course, but in some distant dry season the bottom had been paved with concrete. It was nearing flood state—muddy water with white caps. No matter, I couldn't get any wetter. The current was strong, the water reached my thighs, but I got through without falling and soggily made my way to the Lodge where my wife waited. I undressed outside the sliding glass door. Standing there naked, I looked back up the mountain. The rain had stopped, blue sky was appearing; the summer storm had passed on. I was beyond caring. Numb. Entering the room, I went straight to the shower. As steam billowed about me, I began to warm.

When I told some of the locals that I'd been caught out on the exposed shoulder of the mountain during an electric storm, they couldn't believe that even a tenderfoot would be so crazy.

It was an adventure, however, and having survived it I'm glad to have experienced it, but in the future when I see a black cloud following me I'm damned sure we won't meet on a mountain. Nor am I going to drive through water-filled dips when my wife's along. I still have a question, however, and it is:

Why is it necessary to introduce the profit motive to achieve courtesy on New Mexico highways?

AUTUMN

Joseph Wood Krutch (1898–1970), drama critic for The Nation *and author of numerous literary and philosophical books, spent the last two decades of his life in a country home near the Rillito River of Tucson. There he wrote several enduring studies in natural history, among them* The Voice of the Desert *and* Grand Canyon. *In* The Desert Year, *from which this passage is taken, Krutch cataloged the desert life that teemed outside the window of his study. Here he describes the pleasures of the autumn air.*

Now that the end of October has come, I have assured myself by many signs that the autumn, which might have come unnoticed if I had not kept my eyes and ears open, has arrived in its own quiet way. Though the midday temperature still gives no hint of the fact, I fancy that I can notice a diminution in the brilliance of the light now that the sun does not come so close to the zenith as it did in early summer. I think it is that diminished brilliance, rather than any change in the color of the landscape itself, which makes one aware that the color is, indeed, the color of October, not of July.

The thermometer still climbs daily into the middle nineties at noon, and at that moment the sun refuses to admit that it has lost any of its power. The nights, on the other hand, have a different story to tell. Hardly has the sun set than, at this elevation and under skies which seldom have even a light blanket of cloud, the mercury begins to plunge downward. Many a day when it has registered ninety-five at 1:00 P.M. it stands at fifty-five just before dawn. Forty degrees is a tremendous drop, something which New England knows only at the onset of a phenomenal cold wave. Here it is almost a daily occurrence, and not everyone finds it agreeable. . . .

Those who feel that they simply must have something more dramatic . . . will have to climb for it. As a matter of fact, it might be said that the seasons here are more a matter of vertical distance than of time, for with mountains of imposing height scattered casually about through most parts of Arizona and New Mexico one is never at any season of the year very far from a totally different climatic zone. Three-quarters of an hour in an automobile and less than thirty miles in horizontal distance takes one from the Lower Sonoran Desert, where it is summer even in October, to an altitude of seven thousand feet, where it is, by now, autumn even according to a New Englander's standards. As one mounts, the saguaro and paloverde disappear quite suddenly to give way to evergreens and, in the moister situations, to cottonwood and sycamore also. Even several weeks ago the cottonwoods up there were already as unmistakably autumnal as anything in New England, and all the trees were full of birds, many of whom never descend to a lower region.

This is one of the reasons why . . . there are more nesting land birds in southeastern Arizona than in any other area of comparable size in the United States. . . . It is also why the flora is as varied as the bird population, and why, if one includes the region of the San Francisco Peaks near the middle of the state, one can say that the plant life covers every climatic division from the subtropical to the alpine. In fact, some of the very same plants growing on the mountaintops grow also within the Arctic Circle.

Interesting as these facts are—and I have verified some of them for myself—I have a feeling that to climb for one's autumn is plain cheating. What counts is what is here. I will not consider the mountaintops, no matter how accessible, for the same reason that I would not consider the effects of a journey I might make by jet plane to the Dakotas in not much more time.

But to *look* up is certainly legitimate. The sky above is as much a part of a given place as the earth beneath, and the stars know, if the plants and animals do not seem to, that the earth has moved. This year it so happens that, as dusk falls, Jupiter, riding high in the sky, is suddenly there while twilight is still bright almost to brilliance; and his presence reminds one to watch for the appearance, one by one, of the stars which are no longer where they were at twilight a few months ago.

The fields of heaven have changed more than those of earth. Despite the disappearance of many summer blossoms, the world is still almost as green, with the subdued greenness of the desert, as it ever was. But overhead one will find, if one has not recently looked, an unfamiliar spectacle. Scorpio, so conspicuous a few months ago, now sets soon after dusk, with Sagittarius following in his eternal, hopeless pursuit. The Big Dipper now dips so soon behind the mountains which close my northern horizon that one would have to get to bed very early indeed not to outwatch the Bear. But the Pleiades are much sooner up, and before long Aldebaran, true to his Arabic name, follows them out of the east. Orion, who did not rise in August until early morning, now puts in his appearance before midnight with his belt and his sword between the blaze of Betelgeuse and the blaze of Rigel. For a long time to come they will join me earlier and earlier and soon even the Dog Star, brightest of all, will be visible. Once already, when I was up before dawn, I saw him burning so fiercely that I can well understand why the ancients supposed that when, in summer, he rode invisible across the sky close beside the sun, his presence was responsible for the unusual heat of the dog days.

Nothing else in the visible world can be counted on so surely as these scheduled spectacles of the sky. Nowhere does January bring snow or April bring showers with anything like such ineluctable certainty. The stars' unvarying cycle of changes is the most nearly dependable phenomenon which has come under human observation. Every night they move across the heavens in fixed relation to one another, as though they were indeed borne 'round and 'round on the inner surface of a great, eternally revolving sphere. If we could see them for twenty-four hours a day, the monotony of their march might well, by now, have modified profoundly man's feeling about the universe in which he lives. Even as it is, every season of every year sees them return at a given hour to the exact point they occupied the year before. This, we are inclined to say, is the one thing which can be counted upon, the one thing which certainly always was and always will be just so and no otherwise.

The land harbors memories. In her poem "Fall Reunion," dedicated to her grandfather Andrés, Chicana poet Rita Magdaleno evokes some of her own memories of the autumnal landscapes along the middle Gila River.

In Grover Canyon,
oak leaves curl gold
and the stripped hills
are brown, *cafe
con leche,* children
playing tug of war
on a dirt road.

Earlier, your daughters
laced pink silk roses
over you, a century
plant breathing high
above the weeds
and candles, a simple
crucifix, plots
and headstones, wild
desert, a small piece
of malachite blue
on the gravel road
stretching to you. This
simple life: to get up
at dawn, to make
the long drive here
where I will begin
to pose among the dead,
rearrange myself
on top of you. This
intimacy of fathers
and daughters, history
shaped from the center
of the soul. Late
rain breathing
all around us.

ARIZONA NIGHTS

❖

Coyote, known as Ban to the Tohono O'odham, figures as a Trickster character in the mythologies of many western Native American peoples. This just-so story, adapted from Dean and Lucille Saxton's O'othham Hoho'ok A'agitha: Legends and Lore of the Papago and Pima Indians, *recounts one of Coyote's more remarkable accomplishments.*

It is said that there are three dwellings—above us, here on earth, and below us.

Eagle lived up there above us. One day he became angry because Coyote was always so noisy. He came down saying he was going to take Coyote's wife away from him. "Then what will Coyote say?" So Eagle came down.

When he arrived, Coyote had gone hunting. He hadn't killed anything and was still out wandering around, so he didn't see Eagle take his wife. Later, he couldn't find her and went out looking for her. He got hungry, found a carcass, and began to eat it.

Then Buzzard came and said, "I know where your wife is. I'll tell you where she is and take you there. But from now on, whenever you kill something, you must always leave something for me."

Coyote promised to do as Buzzard said.

They ate. Then Buzzard said, "Sit on my back and we'll fly up to the heavens. But don't turn around or you'll fall off."

"I won't," Coyote said.

So they went up and up, far away from the earth.

Coyote thought, "Maybe I'll never see my home again. I'll look just one time." He looked back and fell. Buzzard turned around and tried to catch him. When they were very near earth Buzzard finally got Coyote.

Buzzard said, "I tell you, don't turn around, and we'll be able to get safely up to the heavens."

Coyote assured him that he wouldn't, but he was so homesick that every time they went up he looked back and fell off Buzzard. This happened four times.

Then Buzzard glued his eyes shut with mesquite pitch, and they finally got up to the heavens. He unplastered Coyote's eyes and said, "Go over there and see your wife. Tell me when you do, and we'll take her back from Eagle. But don't get caught. If you do Eagle will kill you."

Coyote nodded and went off. He had only gone a little way when he started to get hungry. He thought, "Maybe someone will give me some food." He stood in front of someone's ramada and said, "Hey, you have a visitor."

Someone inside said, "Don't feed him. He lives far below us. Whenever I go down there and get hungry they chase me away from their fields."

Coyote left. He went to someone else's house and said, "You have a visitor."

Someone inside said, "Don't feed him. He lives far below us. Whenever I go down there to catch animals they chase me away."

Coyote left again. He began to think he was going to die of hunger. Then he decided to steal something. He went to a house where no one was home and found a sack of cornmeal.

He was about to eat when someone yelled at him, "Scat! Scat!"

Coyote ran away with the sack in his teeth. The cornmeal that Coyote scattered when he ran away can be seen up there now, in the sky.

The Dogen of Mali see a rabbit's face on the surface of the moon, while some Inuit peoples envision a bear. The Mojave Indians of the lower Colorado River valley see a man, as we learn in this story by elder Nellie Brown.

———————

There's a man, a coyote, a man, and his name is Tharavayew.

And he goes around bragging all the time, and he says, "You know what, fellows?" he says, "you know what I'm going to do?" he says. "Well, I think I can jump over that moon! I can jump it, and get on the other side."

"I'm afraid you can't," [the man] says; "you'd better get something, so that you'll have something to eat."

"Oh, yes," [Tharavayew] says, "I've already had some corn and some beans and some things in my bag," he says.

And he said he was going to jump, so everybody got out there, so he ran
and jumped once or twice before he really did, you know, and then he
jumped.

And he never came back.

And then he still stays in that moon, they tell me.

So they call him the man in the moon, Tharavayew.

*The English novelist J. B. Priestley (1894–1984) spent the winter of 1935–
36 at a guest ranch near Wickenburg, where he worked on a novel he
subsequently abandoned. Perhaps by way of consolation, he wrote* Midnight on the Desert, *an account of his stay. Published by Harper & Brothers
in 1937, his book was an instant success, so much so that the publisher,
humorist, and syndicated columnist Bennett Cerf offered this anecdote to
his readers some years later:*

> J. B. Priestley is a disillusioned man. The first place he revisited on his
> last trip to America was the frontier town of Wickenburg, Ariz., which
> he had rapturously lauded some years previous in a novel [*sic*] called
> Midnight on the Desert. But all the simplicity and charm he had writ-
> ten about had vanished; in their place was a string of gaudy cafes, juke
> boxes, and neon lights.
>
> "What caused this horrible change?" he demanded of a native.
>
> "You did," accused the native. "You and your blasted book! Tour-
> ists began pouring in here the day after it was published!"

*For all that, Wickenburg remains a fine small town on the heavily traveled
road from Phoenix to Las Vegas, Nevada, its population not much larger
than it was in Priestley's day, its nights still full of Coyote's stars.*

Let me begin with what I can remember quite clearly. It was at the end of
my stay on the ranch in Arizona, last winter. We were not leaving America
yet, but we were leaving this ranch very soon, and I had things to do. There
was the usual accumulated litter of letters and odd papers to be gone
through, and most of it destroyed. But that was not all. I had decided

during the evening to burn certain chapters, many thousands of words, of the book I had been writing. . . . Midnight was the hour for such a deed.

I left the patio, where we were housed, for a little hut that was my working-place. I remember a particularly fine glitter of stars, with no moon, and with the desert hills so much starless indigo at the base of the sky. A freight-train was clanking down the valley. It gave that long, dissonant, mournful cry of American trains, that sound which seems to light up for a second the immense distances and loneliness of that country. I had to do some lighting up myself, with a torch, in order to pick my way past prickly pear and cholla and cat-claw and other hooking and spiny growths, vindictive by day and devilish so late at night. The hut was in a little thicket. The sand between the curled dead leaves glittered in the light of my torch; and that would be the specks of fools' gold with which all these dry river beds and their banks are gilded. It looks much prettier than real gold. Some day perhaps it will be worth quite as much as real gold.

An enormous silence had followed the train; an ironical silence, like that which comes at the end of some noisy epoch. They kept early hours at the ranch, except when there was a dance at *El Recreo*; and there was nobody stirring anywhere; and not a sound even from the coyotes. In the silence, slowly picking my way, I thought about this Arizona country. The New World! It seemed to me the oldest country I had ever seen, the real antique land, first cousin to the moon. Brown, bony, sapless, like an old man's hand. We called it new because it was not thick with history, not a museum and guidebook place. Man had been here such a little time that his arrival had not yet been acknowledged. He was still some season's trifling accident, like a sudden abundance of coyotes or cottontails. The giant saguaro cactus, standing like a sentinel on every knoll, was not on the lookout for us, had not heard of us yet, still waited for trampling dinosaurs. There is no history here because history is too recent. This country is geology by day and astronomy at night. It offers a broad view of what is happening generally in the solar system, with no particular reference to Man. But it has a magnificent routine. The early mornings, in winter, are cold, very fresh and pure. Then, under the burning noons, the red cardinals and the bluebirds flash among the cottonwoods, as if nature had turned outrageously symbolic. The afternoons are simply so much sunlight and aromatic air. But at sunset the land throws up pink summits and saw-toothed ridges of amethyst, and there are miracles of fire in the sky. Night uncovers two million more stars than you have ever seen before; and the planets are not points, but globes. As I reached the door of my hut and switched off my torch, I looked up and noticed yet once again, with a shrinking sense of unfamiliarity, how all the constellations had been monstrously misplaced. I was far from home.

✜

Koyukon poet Mary TallMountain spent much of the 1970s in the central Arizona countryside. Her poem "Phoenix Night-Watch" captures some of the scents, sounds, and sights of the upper Sonoran Desert, and it evokes Arizona's ancient past as well.

———————————

Growling and muttering,
a jet shoulders down
into the Valley of the Sun.
I remember running to watch
the 1936 mail-plane after dark,
its flashing red/green eyes.

From the country road
smells of gasoline and melted tar
drift with oleander spice
across drenched grass.
Lingering heat arouses sleeping
pheromones of scent.

Betelgeuse peers down
through orange dustclouds.
Baby gecko quivers on my toe,
thinking it's a twig,
I sit so still,
waiting.

I think you'll come again
tonight, Hohokam Indian man,
to guard your hidden treasure—

a net of finely wrought canals
buried in red earth
sifted out of little mountains.

Guard, my ancient brother,
your worthy works.
Your bones lie folded
through this millennium
in the land you left to us
unscarred.

We watch, sleeping Indian,
woman, reptile,
earth and planet—
in mysterious fusion
with desert night.

❖　　WATERS　　❖

GILA JOURNEYS

*In the early fall of 1824, a party of American trappers followed the Santa Fe
Trail from Council Bluffs, Iowa, to New Mexico, where the Mexican gover-
nor granted them a license to trap beaver along the Gila River. Among their
number was young James Ohio Pattie, probably the first United States
citizen to see the Grand Canyon. In this passage from his* Personal Narrative, *first published in 1831, Pattie describes the Gila River, which he calls
the "Helay," on its course from what is now the New Mexico border to the
Mescal Mountains near Globe, envisioning the passing landscape as a vast
larder.*

On the morning of the 13th [of December, 1824] we started early, and
crossed the river, here a beautiful clear stream about thirty yards in width,
running over a rocky bottom, and filled with fish. We made but little
advance this day, as bluffs came in so close to the river, as to compel us to
cross it thirty-six times. We were obliged to scramble along under the
cliffs, sometimes upon our hands and knees, through a thick tangle of
grape-vines and under-brush. Added to the unpleasantness of this mode of
getting along in itself, we did not know, but the next moment would bring
us face to face with a bear, which might accost us suddenly. We were
rejoiced, when this rough ground gave place again to the level bottom. At
night we reached a point, where the river forked, and encamped on the
point between the forks. We found here a boiling spring so near the main
stream, that the fish caught in one might be thrown into the other without
leaving the spot, where it was taken. In six minutes it would be thoroughly
cooked. . . .

On the 20th we came to a point, where the river entered a cavern
between two mountains. We were compelled to return upon our steps,
until we found a low gap in the mountains. We were three day's crossing,
and the travelling was both fatiguing and difficult. We found nothing to
kill.

On the 23rd we came upon the river, where it emptied into a beautiful
plain. We set our traps, but to no purpose, for the beavers were all caught,
or alarmed. The river here pursues a west course. We travelled slowly,
using every effort to kill something to eat, but without success.

On the morning of the 26th we concluded, that we must kill a horse, as we had eaten nothing for four day's and a half, except the small portion of a hare caught by my dogs, which fell to the lot of each of a party of seven. Before we obtained this, we had become weak in body and mind, complaining, and desponding of our success in search of beaver. Desirous of returning to some settlement, my father encouraged our party to eat some of the horses, and pursue our journey. We were all reluctant to partake of the horse-flesh; and the actual thing without bread or salt was as bad as the anticipation of it. We were somewhat strengthened, however, and hastened on, while our supply lasted, in the hope of either overtaking those in advance of us, or finding another stream yet undiscovered by trappers.

The latter desire was gratified the first of January, 1825. The stream, we discovered, carried as much water as the Helay, heading north. We called it the river St. Francisco. After travelling up its banks about four miles, we encamped, and set all our traps, and killed a couple of fat turkies. In the morning we examined our traps, and found in them 37 beavers! This success restored our spirits instantaneously. Exhilarating prospects now opened before us, and we pushed on with animation. The banks of this river are for the most part incapable of cultivation being in many places formed of high and rugged mountains. Upon these we saw multitudes of mountain sheep. These animals are not found on level ground, being there slow of foot, but on these cliffs and rocks they are so nimble and expert in jumping from point to point, that no dog or wolf can overtake them. One of them that we killed had the largest horns, that I ever saw on animals of any description. One of them would hold a gallon of water. Their meat tastes like our mutton. The French call them *gros cornes,* from the size of their horns which curl around their ears, like our domestic sheep. These animals are about the size of a large deer. We traced this river to its head, but not without great difficulty, as the cliffs in many places come so near to the water's edge, that we were compelled to cross points of the mountain, which fatigued both ourselves and our horses exceedingly.

The right hand fork of this river, and the left of the Helay head in the same mountain, which is covered with snow, and divides its waters from those of the Red river. We finished our trapping along this river, on the 14th. We had caught the very considerable number of 250 beavers, and had used and preserved most of the meat, we had killed. On the 19th we arrived on the river Helay, encamped, and buried our furs in a secure position, as we intended to return home by this route. . . .

On the 30th . . . we commenced setting our traps. We found the river skirted with very wide bottoms, thick-set with the mosquito [mesquite] trees, which bear a pod in the shape of a bean, which is exceedingly sweet. It constitutes one of the chief articles of Indian subsistence, and they contrive to prepare from it a very palatable kind of bread, of which we all became very fond. The wild animals also feed upon this pod.

On the 31st we moved our camp ten miles. On the way we saw many fresh traces of Indians, and killed a bear, that attacked us. The river pursues a west course amidst high mountains on either side. We trapped slowly onward, still descending the river, and unmolested by the Indians. On the 8th of February, we reached the mouth of a small river [possibly Eagle Creek] entering the Helay on the north shore. . . .

We thence continued to travel up this stream for four days in succession, with very little incident to diversify our march. We found the banks of this river plentifully timbered with trees of various species, and the land fine for cultivation. On the morning of the 13th, we returned to the Helay. . . . We named the stream we had left, the deserted fork, on account of having found it destitute of beavers. We thence resumed our course down the Helay, which continues to flow through a most beautiful country. . . .

On the 16th, we advanced to a point, where the river runs between high mountains, in a ravine so narrow, as barely to afford it space to pass. We commenced exploring them to search for a gap, through which we might be able to pass. We continued our exploring, travelling north, until we discovered a branch, that made its way out of the mountains. Up its ravine we ascended to the head of the branch. Its fountains were supplied by an immense snow bank, on the summit of the mountain. With great labor and fatigue we reached this summit, but could descry no plains within the limits of vision. On every side the peaks of ragged and frowning mountains rose above the clouds, affording a prospect of dreariness and desolation, to chill the heart. While we could hear the thunder burst, and see the lightning glare before us, we found an atmosphere so cold, that we were obliged to keep up severe and unremitting exercise, to escape freezing.

We commenced descending the western declivity of the mountains, amidst thick mists and dark clouds, with which they were enveloped. We pitied our horses and mules, that were continually sliding and falling, by which their limbs were strained, and their bodies bruised. To our great joy, we were not long, before we came upon the ravine of a branch, that wound its ways through the masses of craggs and mountains. We were disappointed, however, in our purpose to follow it to the Helay. Before it mingled with that stream, it ingulfed itself so deep between the cliffs, that though we heard the dash of the waters in their narrow bed, we could hardly see them. We were obliged to thread our way, as we might, along the precipice, that constituted the banks of the creek. . . . We continued wandering among the mountains in this way, until the 23rd.

In 1986, M. H. "Dutch" Salmon, a writer and explorer who lives in the Black Mountains of New Mexico, followed Pattie's route, canoeing down the upper Gila River in the company of his dog and cat. Here, in a passage from Gila Descending, *he remarks on how precious a resource a freeflowing river—altogether too uncommon anywhere in the United States—truly is.*

Running water of any sort being on the order of a rare gem in the Southwest, what there is tends to be of great interest to those who would either commercialize it, keep it inviolate, or use it for recreation. Those rare, pristine gems like the Gila (I was now within twenty-five miles of the end of the natural Gila) which have neither been greatly commercialized nor overused for recreation, necessarily stand out as the region's most precious treasures. With mixed emotions—not wishing to inadvertently promote either commercialization or overuse—a canoeist herein reveals another river (stream really) within the region which stands out with a similar appeal.

The San Francisco River forms in the White Mountains of Arizona and heads directly for the nearby New Mexico line. They've got it plugged up right at the border, forming a pond called Luna Lake, but a trickle of it carries on, picking up a rill or two coming off Escudilla Mountain and a few others, like Centerfire Creek, over in New Mexico before it runs through the town of Reserve. From there it streams on into the Gila National Forest once again, picking up Tularosa Creek, Negrito Creek, then a good stream, Whitewater Creek . . . at Glenwood, below which it turns back west towards Arizona. From there, for about thirty miles (about fifteen miles on either side of the border) the "Frisco" runs through as lovely a riparian canyon as you'll find in the Southwest. Nice enough that a portion is under consideration for protection under the Wilderness Act. Needless to say, there are those who would do other things with it besides leave it alone.

The battle over the Frisco Canyon is a classic example of easy access versus wilderness style recreation. Although there is no road per se in the canyon a well-equipped off-road vehicle can, during much of the year, make a fifty-mile run all the way from the Frisco Hot Springs, where the canyon begins, to Clifton, Arizona. During the 1960s ORV use in the canyon began to increase markedly. A diverse group of conservationists began to lobby the Forest Service to exclude vehicles and to consider some kind of wilderness designation for the canyon. Several ORV groups, in particular the Las Cruces Jeep Club, lobbied in kind for their right to use the canyon as a road. Through it all the Gila National Forest, managers of the region, has consistently sided with the ORV users—"Off-road vehicle use in the San Francisco River bottom is not at present presenting unacceptable resource loss" has been the standard Forest Service response to the conservationists right up into the 1980s. . . .

Now, in the 1980s, the Forest Service plans to drop the area as a [Wilderness Study Area], thereby solidifying ORV use there for future generations. Of course confirmed wilderness lovers like me will always push for a wilderness designation, wherever we can get it. Knowing we often don't get what we want, it makes sense for conservationists in the Southwest to focus their attentions on the riparian areas. For running water, when undisturbed, provides an ecosystem, a life zone, all its own, a riparian swath of cottonwood, sycamore, Emory Oak, walnut, hackberry and dozens of other streamside plants that can nourish over the length of one stream everything from *Canadian* zone forests down through *Sonoran* desert. It is in the desert regions—as along the Frisco Canyon, or the Gila where I traveled—that the narrow winding trail of the riparian zone shows its best effect, forming a continuous, tenuous oasis that trails through an otherwise arid land and multiplies species of plants, birds, fish and mammals along its route. And so in the Frisco Canyon and elsewhere the battle goes on.

✢

The occasional use of Pima and Spanish words lends J. William Lloyd's turn-of-the-century doggerel poem "To Ride Beside the Gila" regional authenticity—but, sad to say, not much artistry.

———————————

To ride beside the Gila!
　　Loping down the desert trails,
While among the gray-green bushes
　　Scamper flocks of plumed quails!

Where the flooded Gila ripples,
　　'Neath the Arizona sun,
By the Maricopa mountains,
　　Where the Pima ponies run.

Where its turbid waters tumble,
　　Golden with their wealthy stain,
Muddy food and liquid richness
　　For the irrigated grain.

When its bed was dry as desert,
　　I have ridden therein, too;
When the curled mud cracked like pot-sherds
　　'Neath the tread of hoof or shoe.

Where the *awt-koll* lizard flashes,
　　I have wandered far and free,
By the grease wood, and the mezquite,
　　And the *oas-juhwert-pot* tree.

With the dust cloud floating after,
　　And the buzzard circling, there,
And upon my cheek the burning
　　Of the sweet and fiery air.

Softest wind, but hotly kissing,
　　Is the wind the Gila knows,
As it twirls the little whirlwind,
　　Or thro' your *siesta* blows.

Or at night comes cool, caressing,
　　To your couch beneath the stars;
"Mine the breath of leagues of freedom,
　　Sleep on, friend, forget the bars!"

Bahn, coyote, tracks here pattern,
　　Yonder leaps the long-eared hare,
Doves in hundreds coo and flutter—
　　Wild the scene, but O how fair!

All around the tinted desert,
　　All around the pointed hills—
O to ride beside the Gila,
　　What a longing it fulfills!

ARIZONA RIVERS

A legend so old that its origins are lost has it that no one who has drunk from the Hassayampa River in west-central Arizona will ever tell the truth again. In the poem "The Hassayampa River," published in the Arizona Republic *in 1896, John Mitchell, a journalist and booster, sought to reverse the curse of the Hassayampa, and, coincidentally, to stir up a little business for the town of Wickenburg. Residents of Prescott, upstream, modified the legend so that water taken from "above the crossing"—that is, taken from their part of the river—may be ingested without harm.*

"Hassayampa—Queen of Waters."
   There is magic in the name;
It's a fascinating stream when all is
   said,
And everybody knows who has wandered
   where it flows
There's a legend for each pebble in
   its bed.

But, best of all, the story of the
   noble pioneers
Who hailed it a good omen on their
   way,
And those loyal men and true have
   imbued it through
With the Arizona spirit of today.

For the Hassayampa's water is a
   blessing to the land—
(In spite of shocking tales with
   which it's cursed—
That he ever after lies in a way to
   win first prize,
Who quaffs the Hassayamp' to quench
   his thirst).

Salvation of the farmer, and the
    miner's friend in need.
It makes the man who drinks it
    brave and true,
And no matter where he stays he'll
    come back to end his days
In the land the Hassayampa wanders
    through.

*Mary Austin (1868–1934) was one of the Anglo Southwest's earliest writers
of note. Well in advance of her time, she articulated feminist, ecological, and
Native American concerns through a body of distinguished work, much of it
set in the Mojave Desert of California and western Arizona.*

In his Autobiographical Novel, *Kenneth Rexroth recalls, "Mary Austin
was a type I had never known well before, a thoroughly professionalized
and successful woman writer. . . . Talking about life and letters she helped me
to realize that it was possible to adopt literature as a profession with the
same dignity that you adopt medicine, and in turn demand the same respect
from society. . . . She knew people all over the Southwest, especially off the
main lines of travel; people in remote valleys in central Nevada and east of
the mountains on the California line, around the Four Corners, on the Tonto
Rim, and tucked away in box canyons in Utah, like the one in* Riders of the
Purple Sage."

*Lawrence Clark Powell, the Southwest's preeminent bibliographer, has
said that Austin's book* The Land of Journeys' Ending (1924) *can be considered the "single work to represent the creative literature of the Southwest."
In this passage, among keen observations on the importance of water in the
arid Southwest, Austin offers yet another version of the legend of the
Hassayampa.*

Beyond the *entrada* of the Virgin River from the north, the Colorado turns
and widens, the hills stand back. This is the site of the projected dam
which, with a system of control dams at points farther up, all the way to
Wyoming, will convert the river's fury into terms of power. Below the

turns the gorges are of diminished splendor, as the plateau breaks down by less and less steep bajadas to the level of the Mojave Desert. Here it goes with a steady, wide surge over hard bottom. Beyond Black Cañon and Pyramid and Bill Williams, the desert pushes up close along the river. The last of the cinder cones, streaked with white and vermilion ash, and the black lava masses are left behind. Here the mesquite and the creosote line the sandy washes, the ocotilla shakes its scarlet-tipped thyrses against the black rock, and the flat branchlets of the prickly-pear are lined with rose and white and saffron-colored flames.

At Mohave City the river issues between sandy flats under a wide sky in which the blue holds on until well past midnight, and the planets are white lamps swinging free in a twilight space. Below the Santa Fé railroad crossing, The Needles, fawn-colored, splintered pinnacles, stand off to the east, and the *carrizales* begin. About Bill Williams Fork there are many colored walls, and then the long, winding slide to where the river turns about the point of Chocolate Mountains, turns again along a line of black, barren *picachos* and receives the Rio Gila.

Between Bill Williams and the Gila, the river seems to flow as Alarcón, being towed up it by the worshipful Cócopahs as a son of the Sun, observed, on a raised way of its own making, built up of enormous deposits of silt in its retarded course. To the west the land falls away in a glimmering desert basin, the Salton Sink, the logical continuation northward of the California Gulf. There must have been a time when Lower California was the island Alarcón expected to find, with the sea tides racing between San Jacinto and San Bernardino. Then the mountains lifted both together, and set back the sea-race toward the south. At that time the *entrada* of the Rio Colorado must have been about where Yuma is now, until by the steady pouring of its sands, it built a bar across the head of the estuary toward Cócopah Mountains, and cut off the Salton basin. Not all at once, nor permanently. Century by century the wilful river would break back into the inland sea, flooding and filling, until, in turn, the lake water cut the bar and mingled with the gulf again. . . .

Forget now, if you know, how our border runs here. Forget if you can that shortsighted instinct of ours for the thing that promises most for the moment to the interested parties, which we call our Business Sense, by which our border was run in the worst possible place for the future that the land and river promised. It should have dropped from Nogales along the Sonoran crest to Guaymas and taken in the whole of Baja California, and might once or twice, in spite of initial error, have been laid there had it not been for our characteristic tendency to label as impractical any project which knows intimately, looks far, and feels profoundly. But there, at least, the land lies, one vast alluvial plain and delta, hot under the sun, cooled by vast rushes of wind up from the gulf or down from the Pacific across the pass of San Gorgonio, watered by the perpetual race of mountain-seeking cloud-drift. And fertile! After the subsidence of spring floods, the gentle Yuma pokes a hole with his toe in the freshly deposited silt, drops a corn there, presses it in with the ball of his foot, and goes fishing until harvest. In the mountains of San Jacinto, passing south, gold is found; there a kunzite, garnet, and beryl, rose pink or diamond white.

The Gila comes in from the east, wide and slow and intermittent as the seasons run. It drains from the south slope of the Mogollon Rim, east by the Mimbres of New Mexico, north by the Salado to the White Mountains and by the Rio Verde to Bill Williams Mountain and the southern slope of that divide of which the north slope provides the blue water of the Havasupai. From the south the San Pedro River reaches the goal in good seasons, and the Santa Cruz, passing Tucson. Opposite Maricopa Point, where the Gila turns south around Gila Mountains, it receives the Hassyampa. This is a river inconsiderable except that its waters have a virtue by which, after having drunk them, you see the world all rainbow-colored, as all poets and most Arizonians see it.

These things are important; they come down with the river as the silt comes, and enrich the human history enacted there. All this color, the splendor of mountains and the broad lift of the mesas, the river's mighty rages, the drama of the Grand Cañon, the tribal legends, the wild asses drinking at the cloud pools, the cities of our Ancients—these come down to the habitable lands and spread something as precious to the culture that arises there as the alluvium of the delta. Never to the deltas of the Nile or the Ganges, never to Tigris and Euphrates, came a richer residuum of the things that make great and powerful cultures. Powerful, I mean, in their capacity to affect the history of all culture.

THE COLORADO DELTA

Unsubtly advocating the addition of a littoral zone to Arizona's many ecosystems, this unsigned editorial in an 1874 number of the Yuma Sentinel *agrees with Mary Austin that Washington made a big mistake by not annexing the delta of the Colorado River, "the Nile of America."*

The mouth of the Colorado River is fast becoming an unknown country, since the steamboats have stopped running below Yuma. But for its belonging to Mexico, whose government affords no security to life, no encouragement to industry and no protection to property, that country would have long ago been filled up with settlers. The valley is wide, and composed entirely of rich alluvial soil. The climate is superb; the heat of summer is tempered by breezes from the gulf; the dry winds of the desert, lying on both sides of the valley, dissipate and oxydize all miasma arising from decay of the rank vegetation. A large part of it is subject to overflow. Extreme tides rise to a height of thirty-five feet; the fresh water of the Colorado is backed up and floods the country for miles. For rice culture no better land can be found. Hemp grows wild in enormous fields subject to occasional overflow. On the higher and drier parts of the valley grow cotton, sugar-cane and tropical fruits, as well as cereals. For the sportsman this country is a paradise. The lagoons formed by the flooding water are filled with fowl. Fish abound in endless variety, from the delicious mullet to the monster jew-fish; hook, net and harpoon can here find unceasing employment. Immense beds supply excellent clams. At the lower part fresh water is comparatively scarce, though the Indians find it readily by digging out seepages along the bank of the sloughs. Hot and mineral springs are found quite near the coast. A feature of the Colorado, near its mouth, is the "bore." This name is given to a high wave, which daily comes rushing in like a wall of water. It is an effect of the tides, and has its parallel in few other rivers of the world. To small boats, or even to steamboats, it brings peril, unless they be skillfully handled. Green turtle abound in the gulf, and occasionally some of these immense chelonians are captured near the mouth of the river. From its isolation this valley has many plants and forms of life peculiar to itself. But just now that book is sealed.

❖

The United States failed to gain access to the delta, but in a few short years the Colorado River had been so overallocated—feeding Los Angeles and the Imperial Valley as well as other farms and towns in its natural basin—that the estuary became a vast, unproductive mudflat, its water no longer reaching the sea. Godfrey Sykes, who knew the region intimately, wrote in his memoir, A Westerly Trend *(1944), "As an engineer, I fully appreciate the magnificent structures that have brought the lower Colorado under control . . . but I must confess that I have much the same sympathy for my old friend, the sometimes wayward, but always interesting, and still unconquered and untrammeled river of the last and preceding centuries, that I have for a bird in a cage, or an animal in a zoo."*

Nature always bats last, and we may yet see the river return to the ocean. Some people already have, as Rob Schultheis reports in his book The Hidden West.

On full-moon nights, the Mexicans say, after the spring rains, when the ghost of the river is swollen and cold and the tides are running high, the river reaches the sea again.

The river and the sea rise, black and silver in the moon. A mountain of water rolls in off the Sea of Cortez, drowning the nameless islands, the barren continents of mud and sand: rolls up the channel of the old river in the moonlight. Green herons rise from their nests in the thickets, making music like dull wooden bells. . . .

And then the waters turn, and with a tremendous silver noise the river rushes out to sea again, streaming out into the Sea of Cortez.

If you had a boat, the Mexicans say (and I hope they are telling the truth), you could ride all the way from Campo Bebe out to the Sea of Cortez and to the Pacific itself on that black, lunar river.

THE WELL

Water is a hard-won commodity in the desert, all the more so for the indigenous people who, lacking the hydrological technology that permits modern Arizonans to pump groundwater at ten times its natural replenishment rate, had to rely on sometimes undependable stores. Many Native American centers were built near perennial streams or springs—Cibecue in the White Mountain Apache Nation, which lies near a spring called tú *nchaa* halíí *(literally, "much water flows up and out"); Snaketown, Pueblo Grande, and Casa Grande, ancient Hohokam settlements along channeled watercourses. At the heart of Hopi sacred geography is the Sipapu, a spring in a tiny island in the Little Colorado River near its junction with the Colorado. The well at the Third Mesa Hopi village of Oraibi is less significant religiously, but, as Helen Sekaquaptewa recalls in this passage from her autobiography,* Me and Mine, *it lay at the core of daily life.*

Some of the earliest of my childhood memories center about the well at Old Oraibi. It is situated down off the mesa about a mile away, via a well-worn trail, and—as in the old Bible days—was for many, many years the sole source of water for the village. Water was scarce and therefore precious. The well itself, dug long, long ago, before the use of pulley or pump, is at the bottom of a basin about one hundred feet or more in diameter and thirty-five feet deep. The soil is very sandy. At the bottom, where the water stands, there is a retaining wall of piled-up rock about four and one-half feet in height that holds back the sand, except on one side where stone steps lead down from the top of the well. A series of four rock-lined terraces, each about five feet wide, widens gradually out to the rim of the basin. Water seeps slowly into the well. . . .

Every spring and fall there was a community cleaning of the well. The sand and weeds that had accumulated within the basin had to be cleaned out and carried away. This was important, and several kachinas took charge, going to every house and ordering everyone to report at the well on that day to work. It was their duty. Some young men might run away just for the fun of having the kachinas chase them, but if one refused to go he was whipped hard with yucca branches. No one was excused. Kachinas also ordered all of the women and girls to prepare food and bring it to the well at noon that the workers might eat. On the day before the well cleaning every family got enough water to last for an extra day.

Lines were formed, and as baskets were filled with sand and weeds they were passed from hand to hand, up and out, to be dumped far away from the rim of the basin. Little children would go in and out carrying dirt in whatever container they might have—a basket, a rag, or a can. Even at the very bottom of the well itself, an accumulation of sand was cleaned out and carried away. After this cleaning it took several hours for the sand to settle before the water became clear and ready for use.

Nearly every family had a cistern, a big basin in the sand rock that cropped out all over the mesa, where they caught and stored rain water for a supplementary supply. When there was snow, they would pile it up and pack it around their cistern as high as six feet so that as the snow melted the water would run into the cistern. The biggest cisterns were made during the time of the Catholic Priests (1560–1680), because they had better tools. These cisterns were claimed by the village chiefs. Each family guarded its cistern jealously, and there were sometimes big fights over this water.

Every drop of water was precious, and there was never enough. From infancy we were taught to drink sparingly; even then, there were times when we were always thirsty. You never asked for a drink when visiting a neighbor's house but went home to drink from your own water. The sheep, cattle, horses, and burros were watered at the Hotevilla springs, six miles away. There was concern about the future of the village. Were the water supply to diminish and the population increase, what would become of the people? A prophecy that there would come a time when the village would be divided and some of the people forced to migrate seemed to offer a solution.

The well has not been used for half a century now. Sand has blown in and piled up on the terraces, and they are grown up with weeds. Some of the retaining walls have collapsed, and some of the sandstone steps are washed away, and the old well is abandoned and forgotten.

The [United States] government drilled wells when they built schools down off the mesa at New Oraibi. They set up tanks and piped water into the buildings. There are several places about the town where water is on tap. Up at Old Oraibi, they haul their water in cans by wagons or trucks from New Oraibi wells.

WATER RIGHTS

Journalist Byron Halsted visited a number of Southwestern ranches in the 1880s, comparing them with the farms of his native New England. Here he describes a dairy farm in western Cochise County for the benefit of his readers in The Chatauquan, *a liberal Boston monthly. The water rights to which he refers were codified in the U.S. Revised Statutes of 1877, declaring, "When any ditch or acequia shall be taken out for agricultural purposes, the person or persons so taking out such ditch or acequia shall have exclusive right to the water, or so much as may be necessary for such purpose." Overpowering individual farmers for whom the benefit was intended, Arizona's mines and ranches usually managed to secure the right of first claim to water supplies.*

The ranch at which the day was spent is located where it is because here on the western slope of the Whetstones has for long ages flowed a spring of water at which the early Indians quenched their thirst while on the trail from one mountain fastness to another. A spring of flowing water is so precious in this arid, half-desert country that when once possessed, it holds the surrounding land as securely as a patent from the government. A ranchman buys a "water right," and the territory it controls depends upon the proximity of another spring. There are vast areas in Arizona and New Mexico where the grasses grow but no stock feed upon them because water is too far away. The Whetstone ranch has three springs, two near the house, and the third, the oldest and freest-flowing, about a mile away. These three together are worth several thousand dollars. From them as central points the livestock, a hundred head or so and rapidly increasing, can wander for ten miles or so into the valley or ascend the foothills in search of herbage. If a neighbor's cattle get within the same circle they need to return to their own spring for water. A passing Mexican woodchopper on his way to the mountains for fuel has no more right to water his team at one of these springs than to enter the house and take a loaf of bread. In fact we were told that as high as five dollars has been offered and refused for a single drink for a wood team. Once the right is granted, the key to the mountain forests is secured, and in time the ranch is doomed. Clear off the trees, and the snows which now feed the perennial springs would soon melt each spring, form transient surface streams, and the wild gramma grass would grow uncropped by the branded cattle.

FOUR FLOODS

George Webb (1893–1962), a Pima Indian from Gila Crossing, some twenty miles south of Phoenix, recorded stories from his own life and his people's past in A Pima Remembers. *Here Webb, who described himself as "a simple Pima who remembers when the Gila River was a running stream," recounts the Akimel O'odham legend of the Great Flood. Geologists will tell you that what is now Arizona was indeed under water for millions of years.*

A long time ago, there lived in these parts a tribe of Indians who hunted and fished and roamed all over these valleys.

One day it began to rain. It rained for days. It rained for weeks until the rivers began to rise with flood water. Soon the rivers over-flowed their banks and the people began to seek higher ground. The water kept coming up and up and up, and the people began to climb up and up and up to the highest mountain peaks. The water kept coming up until it covered all the valleys, until only the tops of the mountains could be seen. The people who climbed up on Superstition Mountain huddled together and watched the water coming up. With them there was a dog. One night the dog spoke in plain words: "The water has come."

Then the water came over the top of Superstition Mountain, drowning the people who were up there.

The water went on rising up and up and the birds flew up and up, until they reached the sky where they hung on by their bills. The water kept coming up until the woodpecker's tail was under water, and he began to cry. At his side a little sparrow was hanging by his bill, and the sparrow said to the woodpecker:

"You big cry baby!

Here I am just a little bird and I don't cry."

"Yes, but look at my tail! It's under water!" said the woodpecker.

"Well! Stop crying! You are only making matters worse with your tears! Adding to all this water.

Maybe if you stop crying the water will go down."

The woodpecker stopped crying and sure enough the water started going down. It went down and down and down until the tops of the mountains could be seen, and the little sparrow flew down, down to the earth again. And so did the woodpecker.

The next time you see a woodpecker, notice its tail. You can still see where it had been in the water many, many years ago.

And if you are ever southeast of Superstition Mountain, look to the top! You will see people still up there, turned into stone. Those are the people who were drowned during the flood.

How long ago did this happen? I cannot say, but this story was handed down to me by very old people.

The extraordinarily prolific Belgian writer Georges Simenon (1903–1989), half a billion of whose books have been sold worldwide in sixty languages, lived in Tucson and Tumacacori from 1947 to 1949. There he wrote at least four of his famous Maigret policièrs, *among them* Les Quatre jours du pauvre homme *(Four Days in a Lifetime) and* Maigret chez le coroner *(Maigret at the Coroner's). The second novel, set along the Santa Cruz River, was based on an actual murder case of 1948; Simenon called it "practically reportage." In this passage from his* Intimate Memoirs, *Simenon describes the advent of a rainstorm in the lower Santa Cruz Valley.*

I took [my wife] to dinner at the Grotto [La Caverna, a famous restaurant in Nogales, Sonora], where they sang "*Bésame mucho*" to her. The meal was not quite over when an Indian burst wildly into the restaurant and several times shouted an incomprehensible word, as he pointed out toward the mountain.

"What's he saying?"

"I don't know. I'll go and find out."

Some American tourists were surprised to see their bill handed to them when, like us, they weren't finished eating yet. D. came back, nervous.

"We have to get out right away. The red mountain has a hat on, as they put it. That means at any minute huge amounts of water are going to start pouring down, accompanied by violent winds."

I pay, and quickly put the top up on the car.

What they told us is true. In a few minutes, a wall of water will be barreling down the arroyo, carrying everything before it, and there is no bridge between here and Tucson.

I speed up. The sky has gotten darker. Sometimes, we can see the arroyo, which already has a little water in it. There is a first ford, halfway to our place, but it's too late when we get there: it is completely flooded.

"That's what happens every year. It can rain for two or three weeks, and the waters just get higher and higher."

"And will we be isolated?"

We say nothing more. I'm giving it all the gas I can. We absolutely have to be at Tumacacori before the wall of water.

Our arroyo, which we have never seen anything but dry, now has almost two feet of dirty brown water in it. We barely get across. In half an hour, or maybe less, the torrent will be over six feet deep, maybe deeper. The annual deluge surrounds our little house, which does not keep us from hearing the coyotes howling all night long.

Once sheltered from the rain, we feel like laughing over our adventure. Isn't that sort of thing just what life out West is supposed to be like? Haven't we seen it in all kinds of movies, without completely believing it? The rainy season this year is late, but it has finally arrived. We lie close in each other's arms, chastely by now, like sweethearts in a Western, following the doctor's recommendations.

Does it ever rain in the desert as hard as in Joel and Ethan Coen's 1987 film Raising Arizona? *Occasionally, yes. Sue Summers came to Arizona from San Francisco in 1879, and she and her husband, an attorney, became prominent citizens of the new town of Florence. In her memoirs, written in her nineties and now housed in the archives of the Arizona Historical Society in Tucson, Summers describes her first glimpse of the bone-dry Gila Valley and a subsequent deluge.*

The next morning my husband arrived [in Casa Grande] in a private conveyance, and we were soon en route to Florence about thirty miles distant. I had heard so much of the raging Gila River, which I now understood we would have to cross before reaching our destination, that I must confess I had a feeling of fear at the prospect of fording it—imagine my astonishment when we came to a halt within a short distance of Florence, and my husband, with an amusing smile, announced that the huge valley of sand on which we were resting was the bed of the Gila River—but I have seen it since and know it well deserves the name of "raging" as its waters inundated the land on its south bank, bringing the flood to the boundaries of Florence. After the barren appearance of the desert, Florence presented an inviting sight with the green trees bordering its avenues and the acequias or irrigation ditches flowing with water, and so we reached Florence on the seventh of October 1879. In a few days, we had a copious fall of rain. Going uptown the next day to attend to some shopping, I met several parties who inquired with apparent interest, "How is your roof?" It seemed a silly question to me, but I responded, "All right." Going into the store, the salesman propounded the same question, "How is your roof?" So then I asked an explanation, and found that most of the residence property had dirt roofs. I had not known we were so supplied with nature's gift, and did not feel very comfortable about it. It seems in early times lumber was at a premium. I learned to appreciate the despised dirt roof as a great protection from the summer heat.

In 1936, anthropologist Greenville Goodwin collected dozens of Western Apache folktales from the mountainous San Carlos and White Mountain reservations. Here storyteller Anna Price, who lived in Bylas, along the Gila River, relates a lively tale of the great flood.

———————————————

Long long ago people were living on this earth. Then Tanager came to them and said that the ocean was going to come over this country and cover all their homes. Tanager came to where two boys were living with their mother and told them that they must build a great big t'us [water container or olla], so all three could go inside it when the ocean came and save themselves. He told them to weave this t'us out of brush and to pitch it all over outside, so it would not leak. So these people started in to work on the t'us. Tanager went among the other camps and told them to do the same way, to make a big t'us for themselves to get into. But they would not believe him and just laughed when he told them. "What's the matter with you that you want us to make t'us for ourselves to get in when the ocean comes? We do not believe the ocean is ever coming here," they said. But those two boys went ahead and made a big t'us as Tanager told them. When it was finished they could stand up inside it and there was just room enough for them.

Then Tanager said to them, "I want you to gather some wood and put it inside your t'us. Also put some dirt inside and some food. Put in lots of yucca fruit and corn and sunflower seeds." So the brothers started to do as they were told. They ground up lots of sunflower seeds and lots of corn. It took them two days to get all this food ready. Tanager told them to make a flat rock to put over the mouth of the t'us, to seal it. So the brothers ground down a flat rock to just the right size. When all was ready the brothers got inside the big t'us. Then Tanager told them, "I want you to seal that rock on with pitch, over the mouth of the t'us so it won't leak. I will know when the water will be all gone again. When it is all gone I will pick up this t'us and carry it some place and set it down on the ground. Then you must come out of the t'us again."

The sea started to come to this place and was covering all the land. Then the brothers went in to their big t'us. When the water got to the camps of the people who would not believe Tanager, they saw the water and believed. They came running over to where the brothers were in their t'us and wanted to get in, but there was no room for them. Some of the women cried to the brothers to take their children inside and save them, but they could not do it. Then people climbed up into trees to try and save themselves, but the water kept on rising and some of the trees fell over. These people were all drowned and washed away.

Turkey was on top of a mountain [Kelly Butte, south of Whiteriver], sitting there. Each time he gobbled, the water went down a little. But the water had come almost up to him and the foam from the water was right on the tip of his tail. That is why the end of Turkey's tail is white today. Mountain Sheep plowed in the earth with his horns and went into the water and swam. When he came out of the water his eyes were yellow. This is the way Turkey and Mountain Sheep helped those people in the big t'us.

Now the water started to sink into the ground and go away. When the water was gone, Tanager set the t'us down by the side of the river. The people inside it came out. All the earth was changed. All the mountains and trees and plants and rocks, everything had been washed away. At that place there was only level, sandy country with nothing growing on it at all. One boy cried to his mother, "What will we get here to eat? There is nothing." The mother told him to go and look inside the t'us to see if any food was left. The boy found a little of their corn and a few acorns and yucca fruit. They took it out and divided it up equally. "Now where will we get fire?" they asked. Their mother told them to go and look in the t'us again and get some white rock and some rotten wood powder. This t'us was like their house. They had everything in it. She told them to bring some wood from inside the t'us also. The brothers went inside again and found the white rocks and powder of rotten wood and wood and brought them all outside. There was no wood left in this country at all. They worked on the fire and started it up. Their mother told them, "We have some pots in there. Bring them out so I can make some corn stew."

They did not have much food left, and now they had cooked it and used it all up. They all felt badly about this and were sitting there crying. "What are we going to eat tomorrow?" they asked. Then Turkey came to them and told them not to cry, that tomorrow there would be lots of food for them. The next morning Turkey came and told them to start a fire and put a pot of water on to heat. Then Turkey went off and shook himself. Out of his feathers and body dropped lots of gray corn. The [Apache] people went over there and gathered it all up. Then Turkey walked a little way further and shook out of himself lots of red corn seeds. They all went over and gathered the red corn seeds from the ground. Turkey went a little way further and stopped and shook himself again and yellow corn seeds fell out of him to the ground. This the people gathered up also. All the people who had corn went on one side, and what Turkey did next was for those who had no corn. He shook himself and blue corn seeds fell to the ground. This was for the people. The last time Turkey shook himself striped corn grains fell from him to the ground. Turkey shook himself four times, and that was enough.

Then Bear came there. "I hear you have a hard time and are starving to death. That's why I have come. I have lots of food on me," he said to those people. He shook himself and out of him fell xuctco'; he shook himself again and out fell xucdilko·he, then xucntsa·zi, then xucts'ise [all these are edible cacti], yucca fruit, piñon nuts. "Now I have brought lots of food for you people," Bear said. He shook again and out fell juniper berries, Gambel's oak acorns, Emmory's oak acorns, manzanita berries, tc'idnk'u·je [sumac], gadts'agi [juniper], na·djilba·ye [edible seed], and 'id'adilko [acorns]. All these that Bear gave to us are the ones that were growing on the earth today.

"What are we going to grind these seeds on?" the people said. "Better go to Rock Squirrel Old Man and ask him. I do not think he will find a rock for us, but we better go there and ask him all the same," they said. So they went to Rock Squirrel Old Man and asked him to find them a rock to grind their food on. It was all level and sandy and there was not a rock anywhere around. Rock Squirrel Old Man was lying down when they got to his camp. They asked him to help them and get a rock. "You are just trying to make fun of me," he said. But the people prayed to him to help them. Finally he said all right. He got up and put his headband around his head and started off to look. Pretty soon he found a metate [grinding stone]. It was a prehistoric one, and must have been washed there by the water. He brought it back and said, "Here is the one I have found for you people." When they got this metate they started to grind their foods on it.

There was only a little water left in the t'us (not the big one) that they had brought with them, and so they went to Beaver Old Man to ask him to help them get water. When they got to where he was living, they found him lying down, and asked him, prayed to him, to help them get water. "Well, there are lots of you people here. How am I going to find water for you?" he said. The children were crying for water, they were so thirsty. "Well, give me a t'us and I will see if I can get some water for you," said Beaver Old Man. So they gave him a t'us and he started off. He was back right away with the water. He said he had found water in some pools on the rocks. With this water the people boiled some corn stew for themselves. The children also drank lots of water. But still the t'us of water stayed full. After a little while the children of Beaver Old Man came to where the people were and told them their father had lied about the water. "He did not get the water where he said he got it. He got it right at his camp where the springs are coming out. There are springs right there," they said. Beaver is the one that the people prayed to to get them water, lots of it, and he is the one who started the water flowing in Black River and Gila River and in springs and rivers all over the earth.

ARIVACA CREEK

Eva Antonia Wilbur-Cruce was born in 1905 on a ranch near Arivaca in the grassy hills northwest of Nogales. Arivaca Creek, which she describes in this passage from her memoir A Beautiful, Cruel Country, *and other watercourses in the area are renowned among ornithologists and birdwatchers for their rich variety of avian life. The Tohono O'odham who once lived along the creek seasonally are thought to have moved farther west when the Papago Reservation was created in 1916. The Wilbur-Cruce ranch is now part of the Nature Conservancy's Buenos Aires–Patagonia preserve.*

At the turn of the century Arivaca Creek was the life focus for the surrounding country. Thousands of burros grazed in the nearby hills and watered at the creek, as did enormous herds of strange cattle, all of which had horns that were different in size and shape. Their colors, too, were diverse, strange, and difficult to describe.

Hundreds of Papago Indians lived along the riparian banks of the creek. According to their own accounts: "Many grandmothers of grandmothers here born, here die. Much fish in the creek. Much tobacco in the banks, much corn, much elderberry. Much food. Much good. Now white man here, too." And they shrugged their shoulders as if they wondered whether things would be better or worse with the white man in their midst.

The Indians traveled every summer to Tucson to harvest the saguaro fruit and then returned to their home—the creek. The enormous cottonwoods and musical stream were their paradise. And mine, too. . . .

About a quarter of a mile east of [our] house was a wild grape arbor where the grapevines grew at the bottom of the west bank and then climbed up to the top of an ash tree. Somehow they managed to branch across to the east bank where they came together with the branches of another grapevine and went on to climb whatever trees they could. These vines formed a massive arch of green that reached up higher than the neighboring trees. At the bottom of the creek these grapevines grew and made a private, enclosed arbor with a hardpacked dirt floor, a delightful playground for me, and a cool resting place for my mother.

Sometimes the Indian children joined us, and when they did we played for hours, running up and down the banks and climbing the lower branches of the trees, or following killdeer, in hopes we would find their nests.

At one place up the creek erosion had terraced a stretch about a thousand feet wide and maybe twice as long. Here was sandy soil where river acacia, penstemon, and mariposa lilies grew. Desert willows, barberries, and many other shrubs thrived in the sandy soil of the terrace, making this place a haven for quail, killdeer, cottontails, and for the Indians who came daily to hunt them and to set their traps.

In the center of the terrace lay a dead cottonwood tree, long stripped of all its bark. Its thick, huge roots and its top branches held it two or three feet above the ground. I had named the log Pluma Blanca because of a white feather I found there.

Close to Pluma Blanca grew elderberry and other smaller trees whose branches hung low over the log. This shady resting place and the nearby surroundings for a little way upstream became one of our favorite spots.

Just up the stream a brush fence formed a foot bridge over the current. The stream came through the logs and brush and made a deep, narrow channel along the north bank where it gained speed and really outdid itself, wriggling and lashing against the bank. About three hundred yards ahead, a large ledge jutted out into the center of the creek bed. The stream dashed and splashed against it, and here Wahyanita and I threw small sticks for Hunga to retrieve. Sometimes the impact of the water against the rocks sent it flowing back and it would take Hunga along with it. The current would make a wide circle and come forward again, passing the rocks, and finally spreading out on a stretch of flat, level sand where Hunga could regain her feet. She never seemed to mind. She was having as much fun as we were.

Here the stream divided itself into two branches; one flowed against the banks of the terrace and the other flowed along the north bank, leaving an island of white sand in the center. My mother often watched us from this island, where she sat with my sister Ruby. She watched constantly for the cattle, which often came to water. When they were coming she would motion for us to move quickly over to the security of Pluma Blanca, while she herself hurried there with my sister. We would all get under the great log or climb up and sit on its smooth surface and wait until the cattle had drunk and wandered away from the creek.

Aimless play was all very well, but my mother soon began to feel that she had to teach me the basics of country life. . . . My first assignment consisted of only one thing: "Look where you step. There are a lot of cockleburs and cholla along the trail, so be careful." As I took longer walks by myself, I was told to look out for snakes and how to use a stick to feel my way along the trail where the weeds grew tall.

From the top of Pluma Blanca I also saw the smaller animals of the terrace—the birds, squirrels, moles, and skunks, and from them I learned many important lessons, not all at once, but one at a time, day by day. There was the time Mother held me up to look into a nest. I was actually frightened when I saw for the first time the tiny, featherless birds. When they felt my hand near them the four infant birds opened their beaks wide. Their mouths were much too big for such little birds. "They're yellow inside, Ma, and they are blind!" I cried excitedly.

"They are little martins," said Mother, "and they haven't opened their eyes yet. They will in a few days. They just hatched."

Here in my creek classroom I saw for the first time a black and yellow bird take a bath at the edge of the water hole. He came out, shook himself, and ruffled his feathers. He was all black and yellow like the mariposa lilies. "It's an oriole," said Mother. "That's the bird that makes the nest you mistook for a bag."

"But that one wasn't like the little martins' nest, Ma," I protested.

"No, different birds make different nests." And we walked to the opposite side of the bank where she pointed out to me the old abandoned swallows' nests left there since spring. Mother explained how the birds had built them, and to me these were even more wonderful than the oriole's bag nest. I stood watching the birds flying swiftly along the banks, dipping down into the water, and flying up again. They were so smart, I thought. I was jealous of their ability to carry water up where water was needed, but I didn't know how to explain this to my mother. I just stood there looking at her. "What's the matter?" asked Mother.

"I don't think I could do the things they do, Ma."

"Well," she said, smoothing my hair, "you are not a *golondrina* [swallow], you know."

THE TONTO BASIN

From 1870 until 1886 John Gregory Bourke served as an officer under the command of General George Crook, who conducted a series of military campaigns against the Apache and Yavapai. Bourke himself was a gifted writer, linguist, and self-taught ethnographer, and his observations of the people and landscapes of the desert Southwest make his On the Border with Crook, *first published in 1891, a classic of Arizona literature. Here, in arcadian terms, he describes the stream-rich Mogollon Rim and Tonto Basin in the area near Young and Payson.*

The course of those who were to accompany General Crook was nearly due west, along the rim of what is called the Mogollon Mountain or plateau, a range of very large size and great elevation, covered on its summits with a forest of large pine-trees. It is a strange upheaval, a strange freak of nature, a mountain canted up on one side; one rides along the edge and looks down two and three thousand feet into what is termed the "Tonto Basin," a weird scene of grandeur and rugged beauty. The "Basin" is a basin only in the sense that it is all lower than the ranges enclosing it—the Mogollon, the Matitzal [Mazatzal] and the Sierra Ancha—but its whole triangular area is so cut up by ravines, arroyos, small stream beds and hills of very good height, that it may safely be pronounced one of the roughest spots on the globe. It is plentifully watered by the affluents of the Rio Verde and its East Fork, and by the Tonto and the Little Tonto; since the subjugation of the Apaches it has produced abundantly of peaches and strawberries, and potatoes have done wonderfully on the summit of the Mogollon itself in the sheltered swales in the pine forest. At the date of our march all this section of Arizona was still unmapped, and we had to depend upon Apache guides to conduct us until within sight of the Matitzal range, four or five days out from Camp Apache.

The most singular thing to note about the Mogollon was the fact that the streams which flowed upon its surface in almost every case made their way to the north and east into Shevlon's Fork [the Chevelon Fork of the Little Colorado], even where they had their origin in springs almost upon the crest itself. One exception is the spring named after General Crook

(General's Springs), which he discovered, and near which he had such a narrow escape from being killed by Apaches—that makes into the East Fork of the Verde. It is an awe-inspiring sensation to be able to sit or stand upon the edge of such a precipice and look down upon a broad expanse mantled with juicy grasses, the paradise of live stock. There is no finer grazing section anywhere than the Tonto Basin, and cattle, sheep, and horses all now do well in it. It is from its ruggedness eminently suited for the purpose, and in this respect differs from the Sulphur Springs valley which has been occupied by cattlemen to the exclusion of the farmer, despite the fact that all along its length one can find water by digging a few feet beneath the surface. Such land as the Sulphir Springs valley would be more profitably employed in the cultivation of the grape and cereals than as a range for a few thousand head of cattle as is now the case.

The Tonto Basin was well supplied with deer and other wild animals, as well as with mescal, Spanish bayonet, acorn-bearing oak, walnuts, and other favorite foods of the Apaches, while the higher levels of the Mogollon and the other ranges were at one and the same time pleasant abiding-places during the heats of summer, and ramparts of protection against the sudden incursion of an enemy. I have already spoken of the wealth of flowers to be seen in these high places; I can only add that throughout our march across the Mogollon range—some eleven days in time—we saw spread out before us a carpet of colors which would rival the best examples of the looms of Turkey or Persia.

RUNNING ON EMPTY

Unless it is carefully regulated by law, custom, or religious stricture, the human presence in an environment can be terribly destructive. In the deserts and grasslands of southern Arizona, various mining, agricultural, and ranching interests have long competed for resources, especially water. Their contest has ravaged the once-forested land, as this passage from Gary Paul Nabhan's prizewinning book Gathering the Desert *reveals.*

With the Gadsden Purchase, Civil War, and rounding up of most of the raiding Apaches, the westward movement of Anglo-Americans seeking riches reached into new areas of the Sonoran Desert. The human population of the Territory of Arizona doubled in the 1880s, largely because of the mining boom. Fifty different mines started up during the Tombstone Bonanza in southeastern Arizona, and with an ore find in the heart of Papago country, Quijotoa grew into a boom town of over ten thousand people. The resource which these mines consumed on the largest scale was wood—mostly mesquite.

Silver stamp mills consume more than a tenth of a cord (.4 cubic meters) of fuelwood to process a ton of ore. By going back through Tombstone area newspapers and mine records, geographers Conrad Bahre and Charles Hutchinson realized the tremendous quantity of wood cut to keep the Bonanza alive for less than a decade. Nearly 50,000 cords (170,000 cubic meters) of mesquite, juniper, and oak were cut locally between 1879 and 1886 for use in the stamp mills, and perhaps an additional amount of the same magnitude was cut to fuel steam hoists and water pumps. Bahre guesses that at least another 30,000 cords of oak and mesquite were cut for Tombstone domestic use during the Bonanza's boom years. This short spurt of woodcutting depleted local floodplain bosques and reshaped the nature of upland vegetation for as much as forty kilometers away.

In 1887, Indian Agent Elmer Howard complained that Anglo woodcutting had upset Papago subsistence: "The mesquit [*sic*] wood is rapidly being exhausted, being cut to supply mining camps and towns, thus depriving them of the mesquito beans, which have always been one of their principal articles of food." Boom towns at Gunsight, Comobabi, and Quijotoa rapidly extracted the small veins of silver, copper, and lead found nearby, probably devouring all large mesquite within their reach. The towns were soon deserted, leaving a degraded desert in their wake.

At the same time that miners invaded southern Arizona, so did another wave of ranchers and their cattle. Durhams, Alderneys, Shorthorns, and Devons were brought in alongside the already numerous Sonoran *corrientes* and Texas Longhorns, but few of these breeds were hardy enough to persist. Nevertheless, cattle numbers in the Arizona Territory swelled from 35,000 in 1880 to well over 720,000 by 1891. Then, beginning with the failure of summer rains that year, an unprecedented calf crop had to face three consecutive years of drought on desert range already denuded of much of its palatable vegetative cover. As a rancher named Land later reminisced, the results were that "you could actually throw a rock from one carcass to another" nearly all the way across southern Arizona. The unacclimated stock died off quickly while ranchers desperately tried to place their remaining emaciated animals on ranges in other states. By July 15, 1893, when a substantial rain finally fell again, southern Arizona ranchers had lost fifty to seventy-five percent of their ranching investment. Gaillard, a soldier-surveyor visiting the Papago at this time, found their situation to be critical: "a drought of nearly three years had destroyed their crops, exhausted their waterholes, cut off their supply of fruits and seeds, and killed off many of their cattle."

When the rains finally came in the following years, floods were "flashier" in that there was less ground cover to slow their flows. The downcutting of arroyos that followed has been intensively studied over the last century. While scholars are not in agreement regarding cause-and-effect relationships, most have been stunned by the magnitude of the effects. It is unlikely that the Sonoran Desert has ever regained the carrying capacity destroyed at that time. Grasses never came back at their former densities. With reduced competition, and with fewer fires carried by the clumps of grasses that remained, mesquite began to dominate the semidesert ranges as they had not done for centuries.

Along watercourses, however, scientists observed that some mesquites were left high and dry by the deepening of arroyos and depletion of springs. In the 1920s, geologists O. E. Meinzer and Kirk Bryan suggested that the presence or absence of deep-rooted mesquites could be used as an indicator of changes in groundwater levels in arid zones. Little did they realize the extent to which dead mesquites would indicate a major shift in the Sonoran Desert economy over the following half century.

Although mesquite wood was used to fuel steam-driven water pumps in Arizona in the 1880s, such pumps were considered relatively costly then and were generally used to pump groundwater that was less than eight meters below the ground. By 1904, electric pumps had been introduced to Arizona and became increasingly available to farmers over the following two decades. At Casa Grande National Monument—the site of the huge Hohokam edifice—the first well was dug in 1902, and water was only five meters below the desert mesquite woodland. By 1918, the well was dry, for the water level had dropped to fourteen meters—still high enough to sustain mesquite. A new well drilled in 1931 more rapidly extracted the groundwater there, and the mesquite began to die as the water table dropped below sixty meters in 1952. As Ira Judd has documented, the famous prehistoric ruins now sit in the midst of a dead desert woodland.

When pumping occurred near rivers, deep rooted mesquites at first replaced emergent marsh plants such as sedges and rushes, as well as cottonwoods and willows. Yet mesquite roots could follow the water down only so far.

At the San Xavier Road crossing on the Santa Cruz River south of Tucson, mesquites were twenty meters tall at the turn of the century, and the bosque stretched for miles. In 1940, Arnold found 111 avian species and twenty-five species of mammals in bosque remnants that had been badly damaged by woodcutters. Despite the already considerable degradation, Allan Phillips recalled that it was still "a paradise for birds." By the end of World War II, continuous surface flow on the Spring Branch of the Santa Cruz had ceased, and pumpage in the area was already one and a half times the estimated safe yield.

Paradise had begun to dry up. Subsequently, as Tucson derived a quarter of its water from a well field nearby, water levels plummeted below fifty meters, then to eighty meters. Only the most exceptional mesquite has roots which reach deeper than fifty meters. Now, on hundreds of hectares, dead mesquites stand like fossils on the dry ground that was once a lush, marshy ciénega.

✦　PLACES　✦

HOW ARIZONA GOT ITS NAME

For a few years after the close of the war against Mexico, Arizona was an administrative section of New Mexico Territory. In 1863 the United States Congress created a separate Arizona Territory, following a debate that included a proposal that it comprise the lands from the Texas line to the Colorado River on a latitude just south of the Mogollon Rim. Three names were bandied about for the new territory: Gadsdonia, after Secretary of State James Gadsden, the architect of the so-called Gadsden Purchase; Pimería, or land of the Pimas; and Arizona. The last was chosen, the story goes, solely because it sounded better than the others.

Scholars still dispute the origins of the word Arizona. *According to some, it is a portmanteau containing the Spanish words* arida *and* zona, *"arid zone," but this is farfetched at best. Most territorial-era writers attributed the name to the O'odham words* ali *and* shonak, *"the place of the little spring"; this has been variously placed at the foot of Sentinel Peak, in Tucson, and in the Sonoran hamlet of Banera, some eight miles south of Sasabe. Still others trace the name to the Basque* arizonac, *a term that cropped up in an old mining claim from the Spanish era for a silver lode near present-day Nogales and that is thought to mean "place of the oaks." In any event, the area appears in Spanish documents after the 1750s as the "Real de Arizona," and the name, happily, has stuck.*

To these quite reasonable interpretations is added Herbert Bancroft's suggestion—forwarded seriously—that the shape of the territory ceded to the United States under the Gadsden Purchase of 1853 resembled the profile of a large-nosed woman, narizona *in Spanish. Following Bancroft's lead, the anonymous compiler of the humorous* Diccionario Malcriado, *a decidedly off-color lexicon, ventures the following explanation.*

Debe su nombre este estado—
y es un hecho comprobado,
a una india mequetrefe
que como el enano jefe
de colonia desnudista
que metía la nariz

en asuntos del vecino,
ésta cometio el desliz—
hija de sietemesino,
y claro que poco lista—
de meter curiosas nares
casi en las cuarenta caries
de una enorme cocodrila
dormida bajo una lila.
De la nariz pierde el pico,
por lo cual la narizona
pierde pues la ene, chico,
y ay tienes pues, A-ri-zo-na.

In loose translation, the doggerel means something like this:

This state owes its name—
and it's a proven fact,
to a meddlesome Indian woman
who like the dwarf boss
of a nudist colony
put his nose
into his neighbor's business
this woman committed the error
—a stunted runt,
she wasn't up to it—
of putting her curious nose
almost into the forty cavities
of an enormous crocodile
sleeping under a lily pad.
She lost the tip of her nose
for which reason this nosy lady
also lost the *n*, my lad,
and so you have A-ri-zo-na.

THE CREATION OF THE WORLD

In the Tohono O'odham creation story, the reproductive powers of the universe give birth to the Papaguería and the world thanks to I'itoi, the god who lives in Waw kiwalik, or Baboquivari Peak. This version is a close adaptation of one Bernard L. Fontana recorded in his book Of Earth and Little Rain.

Long ago, they say, when the earth was not yet finished, darkness lay upon the water and they rubbed each other. The sound they made was like the sound at the edges of a pond.

There, on the water, in the darkness, in the noise, and in a very strong wind, a child was born. One day he got up and found something stuck to him. It was algae. So he took some of the algae and from it made the termites. The termites gathered a lot of algae and First Born tried to decide how to make a seat so the wind could not blow it anywhere. This is the song he sang:

Earth Medicine Man finished the earth.
Come near and see it and do something to it.
He made it round.
Come near and see it and do something to it.

In this way, First Born finished the earth. Then he made all animal life and plant life.

There was neither sun nor moon then, and it was always dark. The living things didn't like the darkness, so they got together and told First Born to make something so the earth would have light. Then the people would be able to see each other and would live contentedly with each other.

So First Born said, "All right. You name what will come up in the sky to give you light."

They discussed it thoroughly and finally agreed that it would be named "sun."

Next First Born made the moon and stars, and the paths that they always follow. He said, "There will be plenty of prickly pears and the people will always be happy."

That's the way First Born prepared the earth for us. Then he went away.

Then the sky came down and met the earth, and the first one to come forth was I'itoi, our Elder Brother.

The sky met the earth again, and Coyote came forth.

The sky met the earth again, and Buzzard came forth.

Elder Brother, Earth Magician, and Coyote began their work of creation, each creating things different from the other. Elder Brother created people out of clay and to gave them the "crimson evening," which is regarded by the Tohono O'odham as one of the most beautiful sights in the region. The sunset light is reflected on the mountains with a peculiar radiance.

Elder Brother told the Tohono O'odham to remain where they were in that land which is the center of all things.

And there the Desert People have always lived. They are living there this very day. And from his home among the towering cliffs and crags of Baboquivari, the lonely, cloud-veiled peak, their Elder Brother, I'itoi, spirit of goodness, who must dwell in the center of all things, watches over them.

In 1937 Grenville Goodwin recorded this Apache creation story, as told by San Carlos elder Palmer Valor.

Four people started to work on the earth. When they set it up, the wind blew it off again. It was weak like an old woman. They talked together about the earth among themselves. "What shall we do about this earth, my friends? We don't know what to do about it." Then one person said, "Pull it from four different sides." They did this, and the piece they pulled out on each side they made like a foot. After they did this the earth stood all right. Then on the east side of the earth they put big black cane, covered with black metal thorns. On the south side of the earth they put big blue cane covered with blue metal thorns. Then on the west side of the earth they put big yellow cane covered with yellow metal thorns. Then on the north side of the earth they put big white cane covered with white metal thorns.

After they did this the earth was almost steady, but it was still soft and mixed with water. It moved back and forth. After they had worked on the earth this way Black Wind Old Man came to this place. He threw himself against the earth. The earth was strong now and it did not move. Then Black Water Old Man threw himself against the earth. When he threw himself against the earth, thunder started in the four directions. Now the earth was steady, and it was as if born already.

But the earth was shivering. They talked about it: "My friends, what's the matter with this earth? It is cold and freezing. We better give it some hair." Then they started to make hair on the earth. They made all these grasses and bushes and trees to grow on the earth. That is its hair.

But the earth was still too weak. They started to talk about it: "My friends, let's make bones for the earth." This way they made rocky mountains and rocks sticking out of the earth. These are the earth's bones.

Then they talked about the earth again: "How will it breathe, this earth?" Then came Black Thunder to that place, and he gave the earth veins. He whipped the earth with lightning and made water start to come out. For this reason all the water runs to the west. This way the earth's head lies to the east, and its water goes to the west.

They made the sun so it traveled close over the earth from east to west. They made the sun too close to the earth and it got too hot. The people living on it were crawling around, because it was too hot. Then they talked about it: "My friends, we might as well set the sun a little further off. It is too close." So they moved the sun a little higher. But it was still too close to the earth and too hot. They talked about it again. "The sun is too close to the earth, so we better move it back." Then they moved it a little higher up. Now it was all right. This last place they set the sun is just where it is now.

Then they set the moon so it traveled close over the earth from east to west. The moon was too close to the earth and it was like daytime at night. Then they talked about it: "My friends, we better move the moon back, it is like day." So they moved it back a way, but it was still like daylight. They talked about it again: "It is no good this way, we better move the moon higher up." So they moved it higher up, but it was still a little light. They talked about it again and moved it a little further away. Now it was just right, and that is the way the moon is today. It was night time.

This is the way they made the earth for us. This is the way all these wild fruits and foods were raised for us, and this is why we have to use them because they grow here.

WAYS OF SEEING

In the last years of his life, the English-born writer and architectural critic Reyner Banham (1922–1989), lifting a page from his desert-rat compatriots Sir Richard Francis Burton and Charles Doughty, took to bicycling through the extremely arid Mojave Desert of southern California and western Arizona. In the course of his travels, which yielded his fine book Scenes in America Deserta, *Banham often reflected on culturally and linguistically imposed perceptions of the land. The English word* desert, *he and others have noted, means "desolate, unpopulated," as in "desert isle"—a term that completely obscures the richness of life in the drylands. In this regard, Mary Austin deserves praise for having named the arid country "the land of little rain." Following Austin's lead, the noted botanist and plant geographer Forrest Shreve classified the upper Sonoran Desert as a semitropical forest, a northern extension of the lush, now-threatened Mesoamerican rainforests a thousand miles and more to the south. His definition accurately puts the lie to common misperceptions, as do Banham's musings, which follow.*

Ultimately, deserts are man-made in what may be a culturally important sense. The Mojave may be my desert of definition, but all deserts are deserts *by* definition. Not definition by statistics and norms—there are areas drier and less populated than many reputed deserts that no one ever speaks of in those terms. I noticed that a number of people to whom I spoke, especially in areas like the Mojave, would not have it that Wyoming was a desert state, and some were uncertain about Utah's right to the title. This is more than a question of reputation; the very word *desert* is a human value judgment.

I say "value judgment" deliberately: we dub territories "desert" almost regardless of their ecological performance. In terms of proliferation of flora and fauna and varieties of ecological systems, the Mojave does a really fantastic job, in spite of its stingy climate and cranky topography; whereas there are wetter and more sanely laid-out territories that bore us with their monotony and lack of ecological inventiveness. I notice that we seem to need continually to remind ourselves that deserts are not sand, and that "deserts are really teeming with life." The Mojave may be seen as a desert only because it is the last identifiable remnant of the dreaded legendary Great Basin. If it had been somewhere else, it might—*just*—have fallen under some different classification.

Ultimately, *desert* is a concept of, and about, people. The word originally meant "unpopulated"; that is the primary sense given by the Oxford dictionary and many others. That is why the world's most prestigious desert was labelled on old maps *Arabia Deserta,* and why Doughty is such a valuable corrective to ingrained misconceptions—for his *Travels* are crowded with all kinds of human beings, settlements, and tribes. The other common root meaning of *desert* as a verb should also be kept in mind: "to leave." Arabia was "deserted," even if the Latin *deserta* is not necessarily a past participle in the normal sense. The people had abandoned that classic desert, just as they were to abandon the North African coast lands. The ultimate definition of a true desert may yet prove to be concerned with the number and type of people present, and what they think they are doing there.

I am quite prepared to accept that a lone backpacker who believes he is out in the middle of nothing, defying a hostile environment, may be in a perfectly valid concept of desert according to his private value system, or the values of the group to which he adheres. But the rancher who runs his cattle across the same territory may believe it to be a "difficult" rather than hostile environment: if he treats the word desert as anything more than a conventional label, its meaning will be quite different for him, as it will again for the bird watcher with his field glasses or the rock hound with his Geiger counter.

At one level it is so obvious that our deserts are what we make them that it seems gratuitous to spell it out in so many words. Yet we make so many different deserts of the territory we conventionally label so, that we are bound to misunderstand one another. The tensions caused by competition to use the same limited land area are almost certainly worsened by the fact that the contending users are talking about it almost in different languages. Practically the only concept that they are likely to have in common is that there are no people there—which is nearly always a misconception.

I try to think of days when I have been out in the "hard" Mojave away from the Interstate and many dusty miles from any blacktopped roads—and have seen nobody at all. I am not talking about inanimate signs of former human presence; I am talking about human beings alive and moving about in the landscape. And I can recall no such days. There is always a point where one drives the truck or car up onto the side of the trail to let another one pass in the opposite direction. As we drivers pass shoulder to shoulder, we grin, raise our hands in salute, or nod our greetings. But now I wonder whether we salute another intrepid survivor, or fellow desert expert—or whether we acknowledge our co-conspiracy as fellow mummers in the Great Mojave Charade, still playing Cowboys and (sometimes) Indians as on the heathlands of our youth. Does the Mojave, as a desert of definition, define anything more than a set of human attitudes to a particular piece of territory that we have agreed (or not *dis*agreed) to call *deserta,* abandoned?

IN EVOLUTION'S CHAMBER

In 1871, John D. Lee established a ferry at the point where Utah shades off into Arizona at the junction of the Paria and Colorado rivers, using a dory abandoned a few years earlier by the Powell Expedition. His business endured, but Lee did not; he was soon hanged for having planned the infamous Mountain Meadows Massacre along the Virgin River, an incident that inspired Arthur Conan Doyle's Sherlock Holmes mystery The Sign of Four.

William Calvin, a neurobiologist who specializes in cerebral-cortical circuitry—the mechanisms by which the brain enables comprehension and action—rafted down the Colorado River from Lee's Ferry through the Grand Canyon in 1984. Many have made that trip, but few with Calvin's purpose: to study the Grand Canyon as a model of evolution, not only geological but also cultural and neurological. This passage from his book The River That Flows Uphill *gives a feel for Calvin's meditations on the landscape he passes.*

The highway emerges from a narrow cut in the pastel rocks of the painted desert. From the edge of the cliff, the view opens out and down. Far below the flat desert of the Marble Platform stretches out toward the southwest as far as I can see, with the shadows of early morning seeming to elongate it. The Grand Canyon, the greatest evolutionary spectacle on our planet, is on that distant horizon.

Some distance upriver from the Grand Canyon, the Colorado River begins its descent through the layers of our biological history. This happens in a narrow canyon, somewhere just below where I am now.

Hiking away from the road into the mountainous desert, I felt the fresh breezes of dawn touch my face. As I approached the precipice, the view opened to the north, revealing a majestic horseshoe of cliffs, the cornucopia out of which the flat Marble Platform seems to flow.

I am now sharing the viewpoint with four birds preoccupied with their early morning chatter, quite oblivious of me writing in my river diary. The morning sun is shining on the cliffs across the way. The shadow line of the new day starts to creep across the Marble Platform toward me as the earth slowly rotates, taking me with it. . . .

The Colorado River, which carved the Grand Canyon, is out there somewhere in the middle of the horseshoe, heading down toward its most grandiose achievement to make a few more minor alterations in the Canyon's sculpture. The Colorado is not a small river but one of the largest in North America. Yet even from this grand viewpoint there is no river to be seen.

Back up the road, I glimpsed the river by moonlight, heading this way. Yet the Marble Platform seems devoid of rivers, as well as of the trees, sheep, cattle, fences, cultivated fields, houses, towns, and everything else that tends to grow up around rivers. If I sit so that the edge of the cliff obscures my view of its lone highway, the Marble Platform and its surroundings look like a scene from a planet unscarred by humans. Were it not for all the cactus and birds near me on this cliff, I'd say that the view was of a planet untouched by life.

I see only natural scars: the surface of the Marble Platform is interrupted by giant, ragged-edged cracks that descend down into the planet. One crack is the Marble Canyon of the Colorado River, predecessor to its Grand Canyon; the others are the side canyons that lead down to the river, carved by the runoffs of the occasional summer thunderstorms. The river is hidden from this vantage point because it has dug itself a very deep trench during the last 30 million years.

The limestone of the Marble Platform was laid down about 250 million years ago, near the end of the Paleozoic era. The land masses and sea floors were then rearranging themselves into just one big continent, Pangaea, surrounded by one big ocean, Panthalassa. The rock underfoot up here on the overlook was formed about 200 million years ago, early in the dinosaur days of the Mesozoic, when Pangaea was beginning to break up into what became our present set of smaller continents, but before they'd yet wandered very far. As I stood up, I accidentally kicked loose a Mesozoic rock, which promptly fell down toward the Paleozoic. I heard it ricochet down through the ages.

Not only is the river hidden, but even the cracks disappear when I descend the Echo Cliffs Monocline and drive along the Platform.

Untouched by life? I can now see that the Platform has a scattering of desert scrubs, but even the local bedrock has been made by life itself. Limestone forms at the bottom of the ocean when the little floating animals die and their calcium-containing bodies sink to rest. And even the other half of the calcium carbonate in limestone was largely contributed by life: the carbon dioxide, CO_2, breathed out by animals may, if not recycled by plants, make its way into forming this nice hard rock. Limestone isn't so much an inanimate object, like the lava pushed up from the depths of the earth, as it is ex-animate.

The road ahead rises and falls a little as it works its way around some of the minor hills in what, from up atop the cliff, looked like a flat surface. Another misapprehension exposed. I find that looking up from the road is very distracting, since I am surrounded by the horseshoe of cliffs, their layers a pale pastel rainbow of colors dominated by reds and browns. There is no hint of the dramatic in the desert floor. Then, at the bottom of one of those little dips in the roadway, the highway swings to the left around some rocks—and right before me appears an enormous crack in the earth, as wide as a superhighway corridor. There is nothing subtle about the way the Canyon greets visitors.

To the early Spanish explorers coming up from the south, confronting the Canyon must have been a tremendous shock, since they were not forewarned by the almost aerial view of the cracks that I glimpsed from atop the cliffs. Some conquistador's horse probably stopped so suddenly at the sight of this gaping hole that the rider was in danger of pitching forward over the poor animal's head. Once the riders collected themselves and ventured on foot to the edge, they would have seen that there is water in the midst of this desert; indeed, quite an amazing amount of water: probably the largest river they'd ever seen. But getting down to the water is like descending the outside of the Statue of Liberty from the torch to the waters of New York harbor. Then there is the little problem of getting back up again. Such is an explorer's life. Fortunately, I know the easy way down to the water. It's at the base of the horseshoe, a mere 7 kilometers upriver from here, at the old nineteenth-century river crossing place called Lee's Ferry. It is about the only easy way down to the river in the entire state of Arizona. All the long float trips down the river must cast off from that one beach.

Lee's Ferry: the only beginning. Just as we count time from the beginning of the universe, so is Lee's Ferry the place from which all distances along the Colorado River are reckoned. Indeed, when they ran out of fancy Spanish, Hindu, and local Indian names for all the subcanyons of the Grand Canyon, they just gave names such as 75 Mile Creek and 220 Mile Canyon, using the distance downriver from Lee's Ferry to describe the place. . . .

Rivers rarely flow in a straight line for very far, given their tendencies to meander, but for a kilometer or more in each direction from the bridge, I can see along the crack until the river bends out of sight. The water is flowing much more quickly than I would have guessed. Something splashes near the left shore, and I look carefully for more activity. Beaver? Rocks falling? Fish jumping? But it isn't repeated.

That's a different world down there. Many birds fly over the river, undoubtedly collecting insects. Sometimes the swallows (or are they swifts?) ascend halfway up a canyon wall to disappear into a hole, probably to feed a hungry family. Up here on the bridge, one is a spectator, a passer-by in the manner of an airplane passenger examining the terrain below. I've come closer to the river than when I was up on the cliff, but I'm still detached. Literally, above it all. Only the breeze, the smells, and the faint sounds of the river below serve to make me feel a part of the river environment.

Such distancing often happens today. Our civilization takes us far away from the elementary sounds and experiences of our hunting and gathering ancestors, leaves us out of touch with our ancient preagricultural roots. Evolution shaped us from prehumans to humans over at least 100,000 generations; the 400 or fewer generations that we've spent away from the hunting and gathering life style probably hasn't changed our gene pool very much. Our deep roots are to ice-age tribes; although we seem extraordinarily flexible and adaptable, our civilized behaviors are inevitably an overlay, a frosting that may sometimes be spread too thin if it is not well anchored in classic ice-age behavior patterns. Getting away to the wilderness occasionally can be a way of watering those roots, firming up the connection to the overlying high culture, preventing dislocations.

The sun has finally peeked over the top of Echo Cliffs. The shadow line has reached the Canyon. Scattered clouds tower over the cliffs, backlit by the rising sun. Mountain sunrises and desert sunrises have always been my favorites. And this is mountainous desert. By the time the sun is overhead today, a group of us should be floating down the river beneath this spot. And probably looking up at this bridge. Tourists will wave at us. The Navajo Bridge will be about the last we'll see of civilization's monuments for two weeks. There are no roads reaching the river for 225 miles, no fences, no billboards. It's a wilderness, totally unlike the Grand Canyon glimpsed by millions of tourists from up on top, behind crowded railings.

The best we can do—if we want a journey backward in time, to see the mileposts in the evolution of intelligent beings, to take a voyage to the origins of life itself, if we want to try to piece it all together—is to take ourselves to the bottom of the Grand Canyon. There we will find rocks of great age, we will find fossils, we will find the dwellings of Stone Age peoples. We will find the land much as our ancestors experienced it, during all those untold generations when prehumans were being shaped into humans. The dimly remembered world from which we somehow took flight.

Such a journey requires some time. The best way is to float down the Colorado River, taking several weeks to investigate the rapids by boat, the side canyons on foot, the waterfalls by inundation. With, of course, the right companions.

ANCIENT PLACES

The early peoples of the Southwest developed an ingenious architecture that made extensive use of features of the natural landscape, quite unlike modern Southwesterners, who seem to prefer such alien styles as the Cape Cod houses and skyscrapers that dot Arizona's cities today. The Colorado Plateau and Mogollon Rim contain thousands of examples of this ancient handiwork, notably the spectacular Anasazi structures at Betatakin and Kiet Siel, at Canyon de Chelly and Kinishba, built nearly a millennium ago.

Willa Cather (1873–1947) captured the spirit of these places in The Song of the Lark *(1915), the story of a young woman, Thea Kronborg, who finds her calling as an artist in the sunwashed canyons near Winslow, on the southern edge of the Colorado Plateau. Cather spent parts of 1912 and 1915 exploring the Hopi Mesas and the cliffdwellings nearby, acquiring a first-hand knowledge of Arizona prehistory reflected in the passage below, which describes the Walnut Canyon complex near Flagstaff. Her later novel* Death Comes for the Archbishop *(1927) is widely acknowledged as one of the hallmarks of Southwestern literature.*

Thea's life at the Ottenburg ranch was simple and full of light, like the days themselves. She awoke every morning when the first fierce shafts of sunlight darted through the curtainless windows of her room at the ranch house. After breakfast she took her lunch-basket and went down to the canyon. Usually she did not return until sunset.

Panther Canyon was like a thousand others—one of those abrupt fissures with which the earth in the Southwest is riddled; so abrupt that you might walk over the edge of any one of them on a dark night and never know what had happened to you. This canyon headed on the Ottenburg ranch, about a mile from the ranch house, and it was accessible only at its head. The canyon walls, for the first two hundred feet below the surface, were perpendicular cliffs, striped with even-running strata of rock. From there on to the bottom the sides were less abrupt, were shelving, and lightly fringed with *piñons* and dwarf cedars. The effect was that of a gentler canyon within a wilder one. The dead city lay at the point where the perpendicular outer wall ceased and the V-shaped inner gorge began.

There a stratum of rock, softer than those above, had been hollowed out by the action of time until it was like a deep groove running along the sides of the canyon. In this hollow (like a great fold in the rock) the Ancient People had built their houses of yellowish stone and mortar. The over-hanging cliff above made a roof two hundred feet thick. The hard stratum below was an everlasting floor. The houses stood along in a row, like the buildings in a city block, or like a barracks.

In both walls of the canyon the same streak of soft rock had been washed out, and the long horizontal groove had been built up with houses. The dead city had thus two streets, one set in either cliff, facing each other across the ravine, with a river of blue air between them.

The canyon twisted and wound like a snake, and these two streets went on for four miles or more, interrupted by the abrupt turnings of the gorge, but beginning again within each turn. The canyon had dozens of these false endings near its head. Beyond, the windings were larger and less perceptible, and it went on for a hundred miles, too narrow, precipitous, and terrible for man to follow it. The Cliff Dwellers liked wide canyons, where the great cliffs caught the sun. Panther Canyon had been deserted for hundreds of years when the first Spanish missionaries came into Arizona, but the masonry of the houses was still wonderfully firm; had crumbled only where a landslide or a rolling boulder had torn it.

All the houses in the canyon were clean with the cleanness of sun-baked, wind-swept places, and they all smelled of the tough little cedars that twisted themselves into the very doorways. One of these rock-rooms Thea took for her own. . . . The room was not more than eight by ten feet, and she could touch the stone roof with her finger-tips. This was her old idea: a nest in a high cliff, full of sun. All morning long the sun beat upon her cliff, while the ruins on the opposite side of the canyon were in shadow. In the afternoon, when she had the shade of two hundred feet of rock wall, the ruins on the other side of the gulf stood out in the blazing sunlight. Before her door ran the narrow, winding path that had been the street of the Ancient People. The yucca and niggerhead cactus grew every-where. From her doorstep she looked out on the ocher-colored slope that ran down several hundred feet to the stream, and this hot rock was sparsely grown with dwarf trees. Their colors were so pale that the shadows of the little trees on the rock stood out sharper than the trees themselves. When Thea first came, the chokecherry bushes were in blos-som, and the scent of them was almost sickeningly sweet after a shower. At the very bottom of the canyon, along the stream, there was a thread of bright, flickering, golden-green,—cottonwood seedlings. They made a living, chattering screen behind which she took her bath every morning.

Thea went down to the stream by the Indian water trail. She had found a bathing-pool with a sand bottom, where the creek was dammed by fallen trees. The climb back was long and steep, and when she reached her little house in the cliff she always felt fresh delight in its comfort and inaccessibility. By the time she got there, the woolly red-and-gray blankets were saturated with sunlight, and she sometimes fell asleep as soon as she stretched her body on their warm surfaces. She used to wonder at her own inactivity. She could lie there hour after hour in the sun and listen to the strident whir of the big locusts, and to the light, ironical laughter of the quaking asps. All her life she had been hurrying and sputtering, as if she had been born behind time and had been trying to catch up. Now, she reflected, as she drew herself out long upon the rugs, it was as if she were waiting for something to catch up with her. . . .

. . . She could become a mere receptacle for heat, or become a color, like the bright lizards that darted about on the hot stones outside her door; or she could become a continuous repetition of sound, like the cicadas.

SATAN'S CREATION

When he was implicated in a massacre of Quechan Indians outside of Yuma in 1849, miner and entrepreneur Charles O. Brown skipped town and made his way to Tucson. There he bought Congress Hall, a Tucson saloon and casino, and lived out his remaining years as a gentleman bartender and civic leader. He was also, by the evidence of the following just-so story in verse, first published in 1879 and often reprinted, Arizona's most accomplished author of doggerel.

The Devil was given permission one day
To select him a land for his own special sway;
So he hunted around for a month or more
And fussed and fumed and terribly swore,
But at last was delighted a country to view
Where the prickly pears and the mesquite grew.
With a survey brief, without further excuse,
He took his stand on the banks of the Santa Cruz.

He saw there were some improvements to make,
For he felt his own reputation at stake;
And an idea struck him—he swore by his horns,
To make a complete vegetation of thorns.
He studded the land with the prickly pears
And scattered the cactus everywhere,
The Spanish dagger, sharp pointed and tall,
And at last—the cholla—the worst of all.
He imported the Apaches direct from Hell,
And the ranks of his sweet scented train to swell,
A legion of skunks, whose loud, loud smell
Perfumed the country he loved so well.
And then for his life he could not see why
The river should carry even water supply,
And he swore if he gave it another drop
You might take his head and his horns for a mop.

He filled the river with sand till almost dry,
And poisoned the land with alkali
And promised himself on its slimy brink
The control of all who from it should drink.
He saw there was one more improvement to make,
He imported the scorpion, tarantula, and rattlesnake,
That all who might come to this country to dwell
Would be sure to think it was almost Hell.

He fixed the heat at one hundred and seven,
And banished forever the moisture from Heaven
But remembered as he heard his furnace roar,
That the heat might reach five hundred or more.
And after he fixed things so thorny and well,
He said, "I'll be damned if this don't beat Hell."
Then he flapped his wings and away he flew,
And vanished from earth in a blaze of blue.
And now, no doubt, in some corner of Hell,
He gloats over the work he has done so well,
And vows that Arizona cannot be beat
For scorpions, tarantulas, snakes and heat.
For his own realm compares so well
He feels assured it surpasses Hell.

THE LAVA CHAOS

Between Yuma and Ajo in southwestern Arizona lies some of the North American continent's most forbidding desert. The Spanish conquistadores dubbed the ancient route running along what is now the international border "El Camino del Diablo," the Devil's Highway, and for good reason. Ground temperatures in the area often exceed 130 degrees in summer, and the harsh land claims lives, human and animal, every year in a horrible death by dehydration—it's a long distance from one tinaja, *or rock basin, to the next in this most desolate corner of the state. Cormac McCarthy, whose* Blood Meridian *may well be the finest novel ever set in the Southwest, describes the highway in appropriate terms: "The desert upon which they were entrained was desert absolute and it was devoid of feature altogether and there was nothing to mark their progress on it. . . . There was no trace to follow other than the bits of cast-off left by travelers even to the bones of men drifted out of their graves in the scalloped sand."*

British explorer and spy Raphael Pumpelly, who traveled the route in 1862, remembers an eerie sight near the Cabeza Prieta range:

> We were approaching the Tinajas Altas, the only spot where, for a distance of nearly 120 miles, water might at times be found.
>
> It was a brilliant moonlit night. On our left rose a lofty sierra, its fantastic sculpturing weird even in the moonlight. Suddenly we saw strange forms indefinable in the distance. As we came nearer our horses became uneasy, and we saw before us animals standing on each side of, and facing the trail. It was a long avenue between rows of mummified cattle, horses and sheep.

The desert still harbors its share of bleached bones, but also the tracks of wanderers who walk the Camino del Diablo willingly. One is Charles Bowden, a Tucson-based author and journalist, who recounts a meaningful trip through the Tule Desert, hard by the Mexican line, in his book Blue Desert.

We decide to cross the lava chaos, take the short route and the eight-mile hike eats up hours. The footing is bad, the crevasses become so many small canyons with descents and ascents that the skin is scraped and the flesh bleeds. We do not see a single human artifact on this stretch. We are the first ones foolish enough to think a straight line is the shortest distance between two points. Instantly upon leaving the rock jumble, the Indian trail comes in from the east, swinging toward the black mountain from the smooth valley below. We have learned a lesson any child once knew.

The trail lances toward Tinaja Cuervo, Raven Tank, a few holes in the rock that trap the phantom rains and then hold the moisture for weeks and months at a time. These slimy pools are the water in this country and for thousands of years feet have pounded toward them for relief.

We walk into the sunset hungering for Tinaja Cuervo.

A nighthawk moans on a rock nearby. I lie in my bag near campfires 10,000 years cold. Sleeping circles, stone barriers raised against the evening winds, dot the landscape. Bits of pottery lie scattered and a short way off is a pile of cremated sheep bones, one more mystery. This desert offers the only place in the Western Hemisphere where ancient hunters cremated their kills. No one really knows why. I finger the vertebrae off a long-dead desert bighorn. The bone is rough, the surface blackened by fire.

I lean over and adjust my stove. The burner hisses with bottled butane from Colorado. I pour boiling water into an aluminum pouch holding a freeze-dried dinner from Oregon.

Above my head, the nighthawk skitters after insects and behind me coyotes bark in the hills. The stars sizzle in the sky and satellites course across the heavens on their errands.

I rest by ancient campsites in my nylon cocoon stuffed with goose down. Energy systems twirl around me: hawks chasing moths, flames feeding off fossil fuels, food produced in fields I have never seen, space machines slipping toward the horizon. I am in the place of the ancestors but the knowledge in my head walls me off from the world that surrounds me. I can visit this place but I will never know it and eat it and worship it. My energy systems cast a larger and more distant net.

To the north, one hundred miles or so, the Gila River sputters across Arizona, a stream totally consumed by irrigated agriculture, one whose course is often marked by a dry, sandy bed. To the west and north, the Colorado River storms down from the mountains swollen by melting snows and is siphoned off by dams and canals and aqueducts for the thirsts of Los Angeles and the fields of the Imperial Valley and electric needs of the Southwest. To the northwest lies the Colorado delta, a place described by Aldo Leopold in the 1920s as the great wilderness of the Southwest and today a scene of death, a raked-over region which the consumed river does not penetrate for decades at a time. Cutting across Arizona is the Central Arizona Project, a $3.6 billion canal which will deliver water from the Colorado to the central portions of the state where God neglected to put the river in the first place.

Far to the northeast, I can see the glow against sky caused by Phoenix, a blob parading as a city. The carpet of subdivisions and malls and factories sprawls across the bones of an abandoned Hohokam community. And just to the east, I see nothing but I know what is there: the *ejidos,* the collective communities founded on the edge of this volcanic desert by the Mexican government so that landless peasants from the interior can finally pretend to have some land. At first these *ejidos* were going to be irrigated farms but the deep wells sucked up the skimpy aquifers in a few years and salt water from the sea began to rush into the new underground void. Now they are toying with cattle and goats, and soon these beasts will eat the desert into the ground. Already, the peasants have ranged over the Pinacate and cut down the forests of ironwood killed by a drought decades long. Now their new animals will devour the few plants with a toehold in the malpais.

Everywhere I look this night I hear the distant thunder of the twentieth century's rush into the desert, the last pocket of space left in the idea of the frontier.

To object to this act is to cut one's own throat. No one will listen to such a voice. The logic of my time is industrialism and everything will be turned to account, even the hard ground of the Pinacate and the Sonoran Desert that carpets this slab of the Southwest with thorns, sand, and the dreams of people long dead and gone.

I fall back into my sleeping bag and let my eyes drift across the heavens.

Eight satellites steal through the sky in three minutes.

A NURSERY OF GREAT SILENCE

In the summer of 1869, Major John Wesley Powell (1834–1902), who six years earlier had lost an arm to wounds suffered at the Battle of Shiloh, led a party of hunters, trappers, and scientists down the Colorado River from the Uinta Valley of Utah to the confluence of the Virgin River west of the Grand Canyon. Powell later headed both the United States Geological Survey and the Bureau of Ethnology, organizations that well suited his encyclopedic interests. In this passage from Canyons of the Colorado *(1895), retitled* The Exploration of the Colorado River and Its Canyons, *Powell describes the landforms of the Kaibab Plateau.*

September 20.—For several days we have been discussing the relative merits of several names for these mountains. The [Paiute] Indians call them Uinkarets, the region of pines, and we adopt the name. The great mountain we call Mount Trumbull, in honor of the senator.[1] To-day the train starts back to the canyon water pocket, while Captain Bishop and I climb Mount Trumbull. On our way we pass the point that was the last opening to the volcano.

It seems but a few years since the last flood of fire swept the valley. Between two rough, conical hills it poured, and ran down the valley to the foot of a mountain standing almost at the lower end, then parted, and ran on either side of the mountain. The last overflow is very plainly marked; there is soil, with trees and grass, to the very edge of it, on a more ancient bed. The flood was, everywhere on its border, from 10 to 20 feet in height, terminating abruptly and looking like a wall from below. On cooling, it shattered into fragments, but these are still in place and the outlines of streams and waves can be seen. So little time has elapsed since it ran down that the elements have not weathered a soil, and there is scarcely any vegetation on it, but here and there a lichen is found. And yet, so long ago was it poured from the depths, that where ashes and cinders have collected in a few places, some huge cedars have grown. Near the crater the frozen

1. Lyman Trumbull was a leading abolitionist senator from Connecticut, first elected to Congress in 1855.

waves of black basalt are rent with deep fissures, transverse to the direction of the flow. Then we ride through a cedar forest up a long ascent, until we come to cliffs of columnar basalt. Here we tie our horses and prepare for a climb among the columns. Through crevices we work, till at last we are on the mountain, a thousand acres of pine land spread out before us, gently rising to the other edge. There are two peaks on the mountain. We walk two miles to the foot of the one looking to be the highest, then a long, hard climb to its summit. What a view is before us! A vision of glory! Peaks of lava all around below us. The Vermilion Cliffs to the north, with their splendor of colors; the Pine Valley Mountains to the northwest, clothed in mellow, perspective haze; unnamed mountains[2] to the southwest, towering over canyons bottomless to my peering gaze, like chasms to nadir hell; and away beyond, the San Francisco Mountains, lifting their black heads into the heavens. We find our way down the mountain, reaching the trail made by the pack train just at dusk, and follow it through the dark until we see the camp fire—a welcome sight.

Two days more, and we are at Pipe Spring; one day, and we are at Kanab [in Utah]. Eight miles above the town is a canyon, on either side of which is a group of lakes. Four of these are in caves where the sun never shines. By the side of one of these I sit, at my feet the crystal waters, of which I may drink at will.

After gaining statehood in 1896, Utah made a number of legislative attempts to annex the Arizona Strip, the little-populated portion of the present state that lies north of the Colorado River. Pioneer writer Sharlot Hall (1870–1943), then the territorial historian by gubernatorial appointment after having served as an editor of Charles Lummis's magazine Out West, *set out by buckboard to explore the Strip in 1911. She did so both to satisfy her wide-ranging curiosity—it was a part of Arizona she had not seen, as indeed few Arizonans had—and to arm the territorial government with information to fend off Utah's bid to incorporate the largely Mormon area.*

In this passage from her diary, edited by historian C. Gregory Crampton, Hall observes the landscape around Jacob (also Jacob's) Lake, and notes,

2. The "unnamed mountains" are likely the crests of the Shivwits Plateau.

presciently, the effects of overgrazing on the fragile high desert. Named for Mormon pioneer Jacob Hamblin, the lake disappeared in 1989 when a resort developer attempted to dredge it deeper for recreational boating. Instead, its thin limestone seal was broken, and the lake literally went underground.

We were going back through "V. T." Park where the V. T. Cattle Company located its headquarters ranch in the early days of the cattle business in the Buckskin country, and where there is now a forest ranger's station as well as the ranch buildings.

The fall rodeo was going on and a lot of stock cattle were being driven out for shipment to other ranges, for the country here, once over-stocked unmercifully in the day of the open range, is being built up to splendid condition by the care of the Forest Service in limiting grazing to what the range will really support.

Some day there will be hundreds of little homes all through these narrow, park-valleys down which our road winds. Just now we are stopped for dinner where the road turns off to the Jacob's Lake sawmill and there are two pretty little places just below us, comfortable log cabins with fields and pasture under "worm fence" or split rails, or pine logs rolled into line. Oats and rye and probably barley would grow anywhere here and as fine potatoes and hardy vegetables as one could wish. The snow is too heavy to stay up all winter but it is only two days' drive down to Fredonia with its good school and pleasant village settlement for winter.

It began to rain as we broke camp after dinner and I walked far ahead of the wagon to gather agates. This stretch of road toward Jacob's Lake has more beautiful agates than any place I have seen in Arizona; they glistened in the rain and I picked up all I could carry and then sorted them out and reluctantly threw away all but the finest. Many of them would cut beautifully and the color and grain are very fine. No doubt they would have some commercial value if gathered carefully.

I found no moss agates but all kinds of banded varieties in an endless combination of colors, some of them the odd "eye" agates that look like an eye, or still more like half a petrified egg with many shadings from yolk to white and a scale of lime for the shell. I found four red stones that very closely resembled raspberries in color and shape and in seed-like wrinkles all over their surface, so natural that I mean to have them set without any cutting on a silver raspberry leaf and have a unique pin of nature's own cutting.

The forest all along has been fine, big yellow pine for the most part. The sawmill at Jacob's Lake is a small one hauled in by wagon years ago, coming probably from Salt Lake. Most of the lumber for Fredonia has been cut here but the mill burned a few weeks ago and new machinery has not yet been put in.

Jacob's Lake is one of the natural pocket lakes helped out by a small artificial reservoir, and it is an old cattle ranch as well as sawmill. From the lake out two or three miles on the road down Warm Spring Canyon we traveled through some of the finest yellow pine seen on the mountain and passed many stringers of a light sponge-like copper ore in the most vivid greens and blues and yellows. Small cuts have been run along many of these leads but they are thin little blanket ledges and so far nothing worth working has been developed.

The road through Warm Spring Canyon is longer than the one we came up from Fredonia on but it is worth the extra time. For a few miles the canyon was only a grassy trough among the pines where the wind running before a big rain cloud made the tall grass ripple like flowing water; then deepening walls of limestone spotted with black moss and lichens and overgrown with wild vines and shrubs shut us in.

The mountain pines gave way to blue-berried cedar and juniper and scattering groups of true red cedar very graceful and sweet, and to blankets of dark, gnarled piñon pines over every rugged slope.

Though the road plunged over ledges of worn lime rock like waterfalls and kept the boulder-filled bed of the canyon at a swift descent, I ran on ahead of the team, the wind singing down over the trees like some great tide coming in. Asters in all shades of blue, and lavender and yellow *cleome pungens* stood tall as my head, and bright penstemons gleamed crimson up in the rocks. Now and again I found fossil shells in the road, worn smooth with passing wheels, for all this lime country is full of small fossils in several varieties.

Running down grade like some Atalanta to whom shells and flowers were only a moment's stay, I wheeled round a point of red hill and the full glory of the country toward Kanab and Fredonia lay unrolled.

No wonder the early Mormon explorers believed that God had revealed to them a land to be all their own—such a land as no white man had called his home—and in which they should build up an empire unlike any upon earth! The red valley dipped and rolled away to the northeast in waves of hill and low canyon streaked with purple gray sage and round-topped cedars—till the mighty sandstone cliffs banded and striped red and brown and cream like a Roman ribbon pushed the horizon up into the middle of the sky. Snow-covered mountains of Utah hung on the haze, and in a gouge in nearer red walls the slender lombardy [poplar] of Kanab backed the green of alfalfa fields.

The sun was shining over the valley though there was a storm over the mountains behind us and presently we drove out into regular puddles where the rain had just passed, and after driving ten miles in search of a dry camping ground had to pull up under a cedar and make camp in the mud, coaxing a fire with pitch kindling brought down from the mountain.

Seven decades after Sharlot Hall's reconnaissance, the Arizona Strip remains little visited, largely roadless, and often forbidding. Page Stegner set out to explore it in the mid-1980s and offers these notes in his book Outposts of Eden.

I have been browsing in Clarence Dutton's *Tertiary History of the Grand Canyon District,* and for the first time since John McPhee's *Basin and Range* I have actually enjoyed reading something about geomorphology. Dutton's study, in spite of its austere title and the fact that it is a U.S. Geological Survey report written in 1880 under the supervision of director John Wesley Powell, is an extraordinarily entertaining book. . . .

The five elongated plateaus that lie between the Virgin Mountains along the Nevada border and the Echo Cliffs near the western boundary of the Navajo Reservation comprise much of the territory Dutton's survey concentrated on during the summers of 1879–1880, territory through which we now travel as we turn off Highway 89 onto 89A and head across the Marble Canyon platform. The road winds down toward the [Colorado] river over a sloping desert of sage, rabbit brush, and Indian rice grass, and crosses the gorge a few miles below the confluence of the Paria and the Colorado at Lee's Ferry. The parking lot just across Navajo Bridge is empty except for a Winnebago and a Toyota pickup with a "cramper" on the back—the proprietor of which is having his picture taken in front of a monument to the old fugitive *cum* ferryboat operator, John D. Lee, "frontiersman, trailblazer, builder, a man of great faith, sound judgment, and indomitable courage." I wonder about the penultimate kudo on Lee's plaque, since John D. was the only Mormon ever tried and hanged for his part in the Mountain Meadows massacre near Cedar City, Utah. His judgment might have been sounder had he blazed a trail somewhat farther south of the crossing where he was eventually caught, and that now bears his name. . . .

In front of us the Paria Plateau terminates in the farthest extension of the Vermillion Cliffs, a one- to two-thousand-foot escarpment that stretches over a hundred miles from the southwestern end of the Markagunt Plateau in Utah to the Paria Valley. Powell called these walls "vermillion" because of the color they turn at sunset, but in the cloudless heat of this midday they seem washed out, the plication of their vertical surface flattened, and the distinctions between horizontal strata blurred to a uniform hue of pale rose. Dutton observed the phenomenon over a hundred years ago. Without the middle tones of light and shade, "the cliffs seem to wilt and droop as if refracting their grandeur to hide it from the merciless radiance of the sun whose very effulgence flouts them." . . .

Our map leads us four thousand feet up into the ponderosa forest of the Kaibab Plateau, and then (our first fatal mistake, for it is Memorial Day weekend) south from the junction at Jacob Lake toward the north rim of the Grand Canyon. The sage and rabbit brush and cactus of the Marble Platform give way to juniper/piñon and mountain mahogany, and finally to yellow pine, Engelman spruce, and aspen. We begin to flank a long series of grassy meadows where early wildflowers are beginning to spot the terrace with color and afternoon thunderheads are reflected in lagoons of winter melt. In less than an hour we have been transported from slickrock desert to alpine park. Indeed, by the time we reach the National Park boundary a few miles below Deer Lake, we are caught in a freak snowstorm that forces us to the side of the road. Two hours ago I was hyperthermic; now I'm hypothermic.

Four out of the twelve chapters in the *Tertiary History of the Grand Canyon District* are written about the Kaibab and its unceremonious, southern termination in what Major Powell alternately referred to as the "black depths" or "the most sublime spectacle on earth." Some of Dutton's most elegant prose is reserved for that particular moment on the densely forested plateau when, as he rides sedately across a meadow and through the pines, leaning from his saddle to pluck a wildflower from a shaded bank beside a stream, *dum, ditty dum, ditty* . . . "the earth suddenly sinks at our feet to illimitable depths. In an instant, in the twinkling of an eye, the awful scene is before us."

There are two awful scenes, actually. The first (as in *awe* + *ful*) derives from the incomprehensible chasm itself, from the power of one's emotional reverence for the majestic, from wonderment inspired by the ensemble of terraces, buttes, walls, amphitheaters, pilasters, gorges within gorges, that constitute the vision before one's eyes. One's ecstasy, it has been often noted, is tinged with a little fear. A little dread. There is nothing to say about all this, no way to articulate it—except to echo Dutton's own disclaimer, "Surely no imagination can construct out of its own material any picture having the remotest resemblance to the Grand Canyon." . . .

It is long after sunset when we reach Pipe Springs at the northern end of the Kanab Plateau. Once the headquarters for various Mormon cattle cooperatives (whose wards had overgrazed most of the Arizona strip even by Dutton's time), later established as a national monument in 1924, it lies within the Kaibab Paiute Indian Reservation, and on this commemorative evening is stuffed with motor homes, all running generators to keep the televisions and air conditioners humming. No matter. We are headed in the opposite direction, down a dirt road that leads south across Antelope Valley and eventually into the Toroweap Valley, the lower end of which dumps in several abrupt descents nearly five thousand feet into the inner gorge of the Grand Canyon. I assure Lynn that we are not missing anything by crossing this part of the Kanab at night. She can take Dutton's word for it when he describes the Kanab as "a simple monotonous expanse, without a salient point to fix the attention, save one" (Kanab Creek). The Toroweap Valley, however, is a different box of rocks. I have seen the Toroweap from the top and from the bottom—in fact from the bottom of a flipped raft at Lava Falls—and I would like to take this opportunity to stand on Vulcan's Throne, that volcanic cinder cone so representative of the basaltic nature of this region, and hurl a few selected insults at that rotten rapid down below. . . .

Eventually I relinquish the helm and we throw down in a sandy area strewn with prickly pear and agave. When we wake at 0600 after a brief and sullen sleep it appears we have somehow tacked quite far to windward of the Toroweap Valley—in fact, judging from the position of the volcanic peaks (platforms? buttes?) of Mount Trumbull and Mount Logan, the entire Uinkaret Plateau seems to have drifted to the east of us and we are lying in our sleeping bags looking back at the Hurricane Cliffs.

To the best of my knowledge, which is negligible and, I am compelled to observe, utterly unassisted by any of the maps in my possession (no topo maps, of course—too easy to find one's way with topo maps), we are somewhere in the middle of a 250-square-mile section of the northwestern corner of Arizona, about twenty miles from Wolf Hole. Maybe. Wolf Hole is an address occasionally used by Edward Abbey (quite possibly as a joke); otherwise it is indistinguishable from the rest of the Shivwits Plateau—a broad, gullied plain of desert scrub rimmed by flat-topped hills, a nursery of great silence. . . .

There is, to be sure, a lot of rock and sand. But there is more. There is unequalled solitude. We have not encountered a single soul since we turned off the pavement at Pipe Springs. There is magnificent, early light on the eastern face of the Virgin Mountains, in stark contrast to the dark and illegible slope across the valley from our camp. There is a pungent smell of sage and piñon and damp dust that triggers the memory of other wakings in other deserts. There is a walk I take down the wash (while Lynn works her magic on instant coffee, rye-crisp, and a wizened apple), and the astonishing color and multiplicity of wildflowers—yellow ragleaf, purple phlox, orange globemallow, red verbena, the white petals and egg-yoke center of prickly poppy. There is the strong, sweet perfume of lavender snapdragons called Palmer penstemon that I pick in a groveling gesture of atonement for last night's forced march. But the *bella donna*, I discover, has already provided her own bouquet of unmistakable intimation—white trumpet flowers of the sacred datura (nightshade) in an empty mayonnaise jar.

At a crossroad somewhere in Wolf Hole Valley we turn west into the afternoon sun and bump along toward Jacob's Well. The route descends a long gulch spotted with cholla and grizzly bear cactus, both in flower, then begins to climb through Lime Kiln Canyon toward the crest of the Virgin Mountains on the Nevada border. This is clearly not a habitat to visit in one's Beemer [BMW]. Narrow and precipitous, rocks that have fallen from the palisades above us threaten to block the passage, and the old truck bed, burdened with its load of rafts and oar frames, bangs on the axle at every pothole and ledge.

We pull over for a moment near the top of our ascent to look back across the canyon in the direction of the Grand Wash Cliffs. A congregation of turkey vultures drifts in a clockwise eddy below us. The meridian sun shimmers off chocolate rocks, bleaches cross-bedded sandstones to the palest pink, washes the entire plateau in bluish haze. Distant buttes dance on mercurial vapors. Again the text is Dutton's: "There are no concrete notions founded in experience upon which a conception of these color effects and optical delusions can be constructed and made intelligible. A perpetual glamour envelops the landscape." Like staring into the void, it inspires awe—and a little dread.

TWO SPANISH EXPEDITIONS

On August 1, 1776, the Franciscan friar Silvestre Vélez de Escalante, then missionary to the Zuni Indians of western New Mexico, departed from Abiquiu, New Mexico, with a squadron of Spanish soldiers and made his way north to survey the northernmost holdings of New Spain. By the end of September he had made his way along the back range of the Rocky Mountains, over the Uintahs, and to Utah Lake near the site of present-day Provo. A month later his band and he were exploring what is now known as the Arizona Strip from the Hurricane Cliffs to Marble Canyon. Here he describes the ascent through Black Rock Canyon to the Colorado Plateau north of Mount Trumbull in an account that reveals some of the confusion—and even terror—that accompanies a journey without maps.

October 17. We continued our way toward the south, threaded the aforesaid pass from the little valley along the bed of an arroyo in which we found a pool of good water where all the animals drank. We traveled south two leagues [about six miles] and swinging southeast two more, we found in another arroyo a large supply of good water, not only in one place but in many, and although it is rain-water which accumulates during the floods, it appears not to dry up in the course of the whole year. Here we found some of the herbs which they call *quelites*. We thought it possible by means of them to supply our most urgent need, but were able to gather only a few and these were very small. We continued southeast, and having traveled four and a half leagues over good level country, although it was somewhat spongy, we stopped partly to see if there was water in the washes from the mesa and partly to give Don Bernardo Miera some of these ripe herbs as food, for since yesterday morning we had not had a thing to eat and he was now so weak that he was scarcely able to talk. . . . We did not find water so we could spend the night here and therefore decided to continue the journey toward the south. The [Indian] companions, without telling us, went to examine the eastern mesa and the country beyond. Those who went to make the reconnaissance returned saying that the ascent of the mesa was very good and that afterward the land was level, with many arroyos in which there could not fail to be water, and that it appeared to them that the [Colorado] river was at the end of the plain which lay beyond the mesa. Thereupon everybody favored changing our direction, but we knew very well how they had been deceived on other occasions and that in so short a time they could not have seen so much; and we were of the opposite opinion because toward the south we had much good level land in sight, and had found so much water today, contrary to the story told by the Indians, and had traveled all day over good land. All of these facts increased our suspicion. But since now we were without food, and water might be far away, and so that the adoption of our plan should not make the thirst and hunger which (for our sake) they might endure on either route more intolerable for them, we told them to take the one they thought best calculated to take us southeast toward the mesa. We ascended it by a rough and very stony wash or arroyo in which there is very good gypsum rock of the kind which is used for whitewashing. We had just finished climbing the mesa by a very rough black stone slope when night fell, and we camped there on the mesa in a small plain of good pasturage but without water, naming it San Angel.[1]—Today nine leagues.

We were very sorry to have changed our route because, according to the latitude in which we now found ourselves, by continuing to the south we would very soon have arrived at the river. As soon as we halted, those who had previously been on the mesa told us that at a short distance from here they thought they had seen water. Two of them went to bring some for the men, but they did not return all night, and the next day dawned without our having heard from them. Since we concluded that they had continued seeking Indian ranchos where they could relieve their hunger as soon as possible, for this reason, and since there was no water here, we decided to go forward without waiting for them.

At the same time that Escalante was making his survey of the northernmost tier of New Spain, Francisco Garcés, another Franciscan friar, conducted a parallel survey of its western reaches, voyaging throughout southern Cal-

---

1. Herbert Bolton, editor of the Escalante diaries, places San Angel at the top of the Hurricane Cliffs northeast of Diamond Butte.

*ifornia and Arizona. Here he describes, in matter-of-fact terms, his 1776
ascent from the Colorado River near the present site of Riviera to the high
plateau near Kingman and thence to the hill country north of Williams,
where he had the chance to compare his survey with an indigenous geography.*

June 4. I ascended along the bank of the river and went two leagues
northwest. . . .

June 5. I went one league north, and having crossed the river went
down it half a league south. I traveled three leagues eastnortheast.

June 6. I ascended the sierra that I called Sierra de Santiago [the
present-day Black Mountains, near Hoover Dam] to the eastnortheast,
having traveled a league and a half to finish it; and with yet another league
and a half did I arrive at the watering-place that I named Aguage de San
Pacifico [Meadow Creek, in the Sacramento Valley]. In the afternoon I
went two leagues to the southsoutheast, and one other eastward. Plenty of
grass.

June 7. I traveled four leagues east, and arrived at the Jaguallapais [i.e.,
at a Hualapai village near present-day Kingman], who had provided much
game for our refreshment. These people are in the same condition as their
enemies the Yabipais Tejua [Yavapai]. They conducted themselves with
me as comported with the affection that I had shown toward them. I have
them to understand that I sought to pass on to the Moqui [Hopi]. . . . At
this ranchería there is an arroyo with running water, plenty of grass, much
game, and much seed of *chia*. . . . I saw no crops, and so believe that they
subsist on mezcal and game. I tarried to rest me for two days.

June 9. I went three leagues and a half northeast to the foot of a sierra
that I named Sierra Morena [the Cerbat Mountains]; in the afternoon two
and a half, in the same direction. I halted in a ranchería. . . . There is no
water in this ranchería, and in order (to procure some) to drink an Indian
woman went for it two hours before dawn to the sierra, notwithstanding
the weather was very cold.

June 10. I traveled five leagues east, and arrived at the Arroyo de San
Bernabé [Truxton Wash], which runs in part and in others is dry; in the
evening I went one league in the same arroyo and direction. . . .

June 15. . . . I set out up the arroyo, northeast and north. I found one
ranchería of about forty souls. We partook of food, and following the
same arroyo came upon some wells [Peach Springs] which I named Pozos

de San Basilio, whereat I met some little girls who came for water with *ollas* that seemed to me to be made of wood of mulberry (*moral*) with which this land abounds,[2] and that are fitted for this purpose by smearing with gum. Thereafter I went in various directions to another ranchería, where I passed the night, having traveled during the whole day four and a half leagues.

June 16. In the morning I went four leagues northeast and north, over highlands (*en montes*) clothed with junipers (*savinos*) and pines; in the evening five north, nearly to a sierra of red earth [the Aubrey Cliffs]. The Indians who were accompanying me said that the Río Colorado was very near, and already were visible cajones [box canyons] very profound which had the color of the sierra. The aguage where we slept was very scanty. . . .

June 17. I went two leagues with some windings through a rough sierra, and arrived at the ranchería of the unmarried Indian who was accompanying me. I talked with the captain, who applauded my coming, and soon dispatched a runner, in order that the rancherías of the north should come to see me. Men and women came bringing me various little gifts (*regalitos*) of mezcal, with which the land abounds. All were very festive, men and women dancing at their pleasure, and applauding loudly what I told them, that the Castillas—as they call the Españoles—were driving off the Yabipais from the south [Apaches] and keeping them far aloof. They drew on the ground a sort of map, explaining to me by this means the nations of the vicinity and their directions; and even with admiration did they rejoice when on their own map I showed them my route, we understanding each other in this way reciprocally. By this means was I enabled to acquire a clear understanding of the situation of all the nations.

2. The mulberry was not present in northern Arizona in Garcés's time. He may have meant the large hackberry groves of the region.

VISIONS OF THE PLATEAU

✦

The homelands of the Hopi and Navajo peoples have been described by many writers, though few as expressively as Creek poet Joy Harjo, whose book of prose poems Secrets from the Center of the World *evokes the beauty of this vast, oceanic land.*

Near Round Rock is a point of balance between two red stars. Here you may enter galactic memory, disguised as a whirlpool of sand, and discover you are pure event mixed with water, occurring in time and space, as sheep, a few goats, graze, keep watch nearby.

•   •   •

A summer storm reveals the dreaming place of bears. But you cannot see their shaggy dreams of fish and berries, any land signs supporting evidence of bears, or any bears at all. What is revealed in the soaked rich earth, forked waters, and fence line shared with patient stones is the possibility of everything you can't see.

•   •   •

It's true the landscape forms the mind. If I stand here long enough I'll learn how to sing. None of that country & western heartbreak stuff, or operatic duels, but something cool as the blues, or close to the sound of a Navajo woman singing early in the morning.

•   •   •

Scarlet bluffs gather here to drink and watch deer trip down in dusk. Everything arrives perfectly in time, including snow clouds that bless the earth. And the moon, the blind eye of an ancient mountain lion who shifts his bones on a starry branch.

❖

N. Scott Momaday, author of the Pulitzer Prize–winning novel House Made of Dawn—*its title taken from the Navajo night chant that opens this anthology—describes the area around Monument Valley in his memoir* The Names.

———————————

Monument Valley: red to blue; great violet shadows, planes and prisms of light. Once, from a window in the wall of a canyon, I saw men on horseback, far below, two of them, moving slowly into gloaming, and they were singing. They were so far away that I could only barely see them, and their small, clear voices lay very lightly and for a long time on the distance between us.

The valley is vast. When you look out over it, it does not occur to you that there is an end to it. You see the monoliths that stand away in space, and you imagine that you have come upon eternity. They do not appear to exist in time. You think: I see that time comes to an end on this side of the rock, and on the other side there is nothing forever. I believe that only in *diné bizaad,* the Navajo language, which is endless, can this place be described, or even indicated in its true character. Just there is the center of an intricate geology, a whole and unique landscape which includes Utah, Colorado, Arizona, and New Mexico. The most brilliant colors in the earth are there, I believe, and the most beautiful and extraordinary land forms—and surely the coldest, clearest air, which is run through with pure light.

George Blueeyes, a member of the Táaahi clan of the Navajo tribe, was born near Rock Point in 1900. He worked as a herder throughout the northern part of the Navajo Nation and later trained as a medicine man and singer. In "Earth, Our Mother," which is reminiscent of the mountain chant that follows, Blueeyes explains the relation of his people to the Earth, a central tenet of Navajo cosmology.

———————————

We say Nahasdzáán Shimá:
Earth, My Mother.
We are made from her.
Even though she takes us daily,
We will become part of her again.
For we ARE her.

The Earth is Our Mother.
The Sky is Our Father.
Just as a man gives his wife beautiful things to wear,
So Our Father Sky does the same.
He sends rain down on Mother Earth,
And because of the rain the plants grow,
And flowers appear of many different colors.
She in turn provides food for him.

He dresses her as a man would dress his woman.
He moves clouds and male rain.
He moves dark mists and female rain.
Dark mists cloak the ground,
And plants grow with many colored blossoms.

The plants with colored blossoms are her dress.
It wears out. Yes, the earth's cover wears out.
The plants ripen and fade away in the fall.
Then in the spring when the rains come again,
Mother Earth once again puts on her finery.
The plants are restored again in beauty.
This is what the stories of the Elders say.

*In traditional belief, the Navajo universe, Diné Bikéyah, is bounded by
sacred mountains: the San Francisco Peaks behind Flagstaff, Arizona;
Mount Taylor, Huerfano Peak, and Gobernador Knob, in western New
Mexico; and Hesperus Peak and Blanca Peak in the San Juan Mountains of
southwestern Colorado. The Mountain Chant commemorates these holy
landforms.*

The mountain to the East is Sis na' jin.
It is standing out.
The strong White Bead is standing out,
A living mountain is standing out.
The Chief of the Mountain is standing out.
Like the Most High Power he is standing out,
Like the Most High Power Whose Ways Are Beautiful he is
     standing out.

It stands out.
It stands out.
It stands out.

The mountain to the south is Tso dzil.
It is standing out.
The strong Turquoise is standing out,
A living mountain is standing out.
The Chief of the Mountain is standing out.
Like the Most High Power he is standing out,
Like the Most High Power Whose Ways Are Beautiful he is
     standing out.

It stands out.
It stands out.
It stands out.

The mountain to the West is Dook oslid.
It is standing out.
The strong White Shell is standing out,
A living mountain is standing out.
The Chief of the Mountain is standing out.
Like the Most High Power he is standing out,
Like the Most High Power Whose Ways Are Beautiful he is
     standing out.

It stands out.
It stands out.
It stands out.

The mountain to the north is Debe'ntsa.
It is standing out.
The strong Jet is standing out,
A living mountain is standing out.
The Chief of the Mountain is standing out.
Like the Most High Power he is standing out,
Like the Most High Power Whose Ways Are Beautiful he is
    standing out.

It stands out.
It stands out.
It stands out.

The mountain in the Center is Dzil na'odili.
It is standing out.
The strong Beautiful Goods is standing out,
A living mountain is standing out.
The Chief of the Mountain is standing out.
Like the Most High Power he is standing out,
Like the Most High Power Whose Ways Are Beautiful he is
    standing out.

It stands out.
It stands out.
It stands out.

*The mythographer Joseph Campbell once remarked that Canyon de Chelly
was to his mind the earth's most sacred spot. Certainly it is one of the
loveliest. Acoma poet Simon Ortiz captures its mystery and beauty in his
poem "Canyon de Chelly."*

Lie on your back on stone,
the stone carved to fit
the shape of yourself.

Who made it like this,
knowing that I would be along
in a million years and look
at the sky being blue forever?

My son is near me. He sits
and turns on his butt
and crawls over to stones,
picks one up and holds it,
and then puts it in his mouth.
The taste of stone.
What is it but stone,
the earth in your mouth.
You, son, are tasting forever.

We walk to the edge of cliff
and look down into the canyon.
On this side, we cannot see
the bottom cliffedge but looking
further out, we see fields,
sand furrows, cottonwoods.
In winter, they are softly gray.
The cliffs' shadows are distant,
hundreds of feet below;
we cannot see our own shadows.
The wind moves softly into us.
My son laughs with the wind;
he gasps and laughs.

We find gray root, old wood,
so old, with curious twists
in it, curving back into curves,
juniper, pinon, or something
with hard, red berries in spring.
You taste them, and they are sweet
and bitter, the berries a delicacy
for bluejays. The plant rooted
fragilely in a sandy place
by a canyon wall, the sun bathing
shiny, pointed leaves.

My son touches the root carefully,
aware of its ancient quality.
He lays his soft, small fingers on it
and looks at me for information.
I tell him: wood, an old root,
and around it, the earth, ourselves.

*Naturalist John Muir, who lived in the Petrified Forest for a few months in
1905 and 1906, and whose efforts helped establish a national park there
some years later, found the Painted Desert memorably beautiful. Filmmaker
Robert E. Sherwood depicted it as a place of howling terror, where a young
Bette Davis was threatened as much by the elements as by Humphrey
Bogart's sinister Duke Mantee. Richard Hinton, a perceptive observer of
Arizona's landscapes, found it a mix of both. This description is from his
Hand-Book to Arizona.*

This is a land of marvels. Between the Moqui [Hopi] villages and the lower
portion of the Little Colorado lies the "Painted Desert," a "thing of
beauty" but by no means "a joy forever." It would look much better from
a railroad train than from a mule's back, extreme thirst not favoring
aesthetics. It is the beauty of death, with a mimicry of life. Here are
thousands of colossal columns, the remains of layers of earth of great
thickness, carried away by slow denudations extending over many eras
and leaving behind these land-marks of their former extent. The columns
are streaked with bright red layers, the deep color being attributed to the
oxydation of particles of feldspar in the granite from which the sedimen-
tary rocks of which these columns are composed were obtained. From
these red layers the desert derives its name. The Moqui Indians, however,
have another name for it, based on another class of marvels reaching
towards the shadowy realm. It has a combination of the "Fata Morgana"
and the ordinary mirage of the African and Arabian deserts, superior to
these latter in variety, distinctness and beauty, combining with them the
"Fata Morgana" peculiar to some portions of the Mediterranean. On its
air are depicted "palaces, hanging gardens, terraces, colonades, temples,

fountains, lakes, fortifications with flags flying on their ramparts, inverted houses, towers, walled towns on conical hills with flags flying on their roofs, beautiful lawns and promenades, landscapes, spacious woods, groves, orchards, meadows with companies of men and women, and herds of cattle, deer and antelope, standing, walking, lying, etc., and all painted with such an admirable mixture of light and shade that it is impossible to form an adequate conception of the picture without seeing it." What wonder is it that this combination of Sahara and the Mediterranean should be termed by the Indians "Assa-ma-unda," or the country of the departed spirit.

In the manner of the bourgeois British traveler he professed to despise, D. H. Lawrence (1885–1930) found something to displease him wherever he went—the food, the people, the scenery. Here he grumbles at his journey to the Hopi Mesas, his repeated vocabulary of color terms more appropriate to Yorkshire than to the Colorado Plateau.

The Hopi country is in Arizona, next the Navajo country, and some seventy miles north of the Santa Fé railroad. The Hopis are Pueblo Indians, village Indians, so their reservation is not large. It consists of a square track of greyish, unappetising desert, out of which rise three tall arid mesas, broken off in ragged pallid rock. On the top of the mesas perch the ragged, broken, greyish pueblos, identical with the mesas on which they stand.

The nearest village, Walpi, stands in half-ruin high, high on a narrow rock-top where no leaf of life ever was tender. It is all grey, utterly grey, utterly pallid stone and dust, and very narrow. Below it all the stark light of the dry Arizona sun.

Walpi is called the 'first mesa'. And it is at the far edge of Walpi you see the withered beaks and claws and bones of sacrificed eagles, in a rock-cleft under the sky. They sacrifice an eagle each year, on the brink, by rolling him out and crushing him so as to shed no blood. Then they drop his remains down the dry cleft in the promontory's farthest grey tip.

The trail winds on, utterly bumpy and horrible, for thirty miles, past the second mesa, where Chimopova [Shimopovi] is, on to the third mesa. And on the Sunday afternoon of August 17th [1924] black automobile after automobile lurched and crawled across the grey desert, where low, grey, sage-scrub was coming to pallid yellow. Black hood followed crawling after black hood, like a funeral cortège. The motor-cars, with all the tourists wending their way to the third and farthest mesa, thirty miles across this dismal desert where an odd water-windmill spun, and odd patches of corn blew in the strong desert wind, like dark-green women with fringed shawls blowing and fluttering, not far from the foot of the great, grey, up-piled mesa.

SOLITAIRE

Edward Abbey (1927–1989) defined the modern desert rat. A fierce champion of wilderness, he worked for sixteen years as a park ranger and fire lookout at places like Organ Pipe Cactus National Monument, Aztec Peak in the Mazatzal Mountains Wilderness, and the North Rim of the Grand Canyon, all the while crafting a series of novels and books of essays, among them Black Sun, Abbey's Road, *and* The Monkey Wrench Gang.

Abbey liked to head out alone on marches through the Lechuguilla Desert, climbs in the Cabeza Prieta, amblings over the Colorado Plateau. In this passage from Desert Solitaire, *his aptly named and best-known book of nonfiction, Abbey recounts a dangerous moment in the Grand Canyon.*

Most of my wandering in the desert I've done alone. Not so much from choice as from necessity—I generally prefer to go into places where no one else wants to go. I find that in contemplating the natural world my pleasure is greater if there are not too many others contemplating it with me, at the same time. However, there are special hazards in traveling alone. Your chances of dying, in case of sickness or accident, are much improved, simply because there is no one around to go for help.

Exploring a side canyon off Havasu Canyon one day, I was unable to resist the temptation to climb up out of it onto what corresponds in that region to the Tonto Bench. Late in the afternoon I realized that I would not have enough time to get back to my camp before dark, unless I could find a much shorter route than the one by which I had come. I looked for a shortcut.

Nearby was another little side canyon which appeared to lead down into Havasu Canyon. It was a steep, shadowy, extremely narrow defile with the usual meandering course and overhanging walls; from where I stood, near its head, I could not tell if the route was feasible all the way down to the floor of the main canyon. I had no rope with me—only my walking stick. But I was hungry and thirsty, as always. I started down.

For a while everything went well. The floor of the little canyon began as a bed of dry sand, scattered with rocks. Farther down a few boulders were wedged between the walls; I climbed over and under them. Then the canyon took on the slickrock character—smooth, sheer, slippery sandstone carved by erosion into a series of scoops and potholes which got bigger as I descended. In some of these basins there was a little water left over from the last flood, warm and fetid water under an oily-looking scum, condensed by prolonged evaporation to a sort of broth, rich in dead and dying organisms. My canteen was empty and I was very thirsty but I felt that I could wait.

I came to a lip on the canyon floor which overhung by twelve feet the largest so far of these stagnant pools. On each side rose the canyon walls, roughly perpendicular. There was no way to continue except by dropping into the pool. I hesitated. Beyond this point there could hardly be any returning, yet the main canyon was still not visible below. Obviously the only sensible thing to do was to turn back. Instead, I edged over the lip of stone and dropped feet first into the water.

Deeper than I expected. The warm, thick fluid came up and closed over my head as my feet touched the muck at the bottom. I had to swim to the farther side. And here I found myself on the verge of another drop-off, with one more huge bowl of green soup below.

This drop-off was about the same height as the one before, but not overhanging. It resembled a children's playground slide, concave and S-curved, only steeper, wider, with a vertical pitch in the middle. It did not lead directly into the water but ended in a series of steplike ledges above the pool. Beyond the pool lay another edge, another drop-off into an unknown depth. Again I paused, and for a much longer time. But I no longer had the option of turning around and going back. I eased myself into the chute and let go of everything—except my faithful stick.

I hit rock bottom hard, but without any physical injury. I swam the stinking pond dog-paddle style, pushing the heavy scum away from my face, and crawled out on the far side to see what my fate was going to be.

Fatal. Death by starvation, slow and tedious. For I was looking straight down an overhanging cliff to a rubble pile of broken rocks eighty feet below.

After the first wave of utter panic had passed I began to try to think. First of all I was not going to die immediately, unless another flash flood came down the gorge; there was the pond of stagnant water on hand to save me from thirst and a man can live, they say, for thirty days or more without food. My sun-bleached bones, dramatically sprawled at the bottom of the chasm, would provide the diversion of the picturesque for future wanderers—if any human ever came this way again.

My second thought was to yell for help, although I knew very well there could be no other human being within miles. I even tried it but the sound of that anxious shout, cut short in the dead air within the canyon walls, was so inhuman, so detached as it seemed from myself, that it terrified me and I didn't attempt it again.

I thought of tearing my clothes into strips and plaiting a rope. But what was I wearing?—boots, socks, a pair of old and ragged blue jeans, a flimsy T-shirt, an ancient and rotten sombrero of straw. Not a chance of weaving such a wardrobe into a rope eighty feet long, or even twenty feet long.

How about a signal fire? There was nothing to burn but my clothes; not a tree, not a shrub, not even a weed grew in this stony cul-de-sac. Even if I burned my clothing the chances of the smoke being seen by some Huala-pai Indian high on the south rim were very small; and if he did see the smoke, what then? He'd shrug his shoulders, sigh, and take another pull from his Tokay bottle. Furthermore, without clothes, the sun would soon bake me to death.

There was only one thing I could do. I had a tiny notebook in my hip pocket and a stub of pencil. When these dried out I could at least record my final thoughts. I would have plenty of time to write not only my epitaph but my own elegy.

But not yet.

There were a few loose stones scattered about the edge of the pool. Taking the biggest first, I swam with it back to the foot of the slickrock chute and placed it there. One by one I brought the others and made a shaky little pile about two feet high leaning against the chute. Hopeless, of course, but there was nothing else to do. I stood on the top of the pile and stretched upward, straining my arms to their utmost limit and groped with fingers and fingernails for a hold on something firm. There was nothing. I crept back down. I began to cry. It was easy. All alone, I didn't have to be brave.

Through the tears I noticed my old walking stick lying nearby. I took it and stood it on the most solid stone in the pile, behind the two topmost stones. I took off my boots, tied them together and hung them around my neck, on my back. I got up on the little pile again and lifted one leg and set my big toe on the top of the stick. This could never work. Slowly and painfully, leaning as much of my weight as I could against the sandstone slide, I applied more and more pressure to the stick, pushing my body upward until I was again stretched out full length above it. Again I felt about for a fingerhold. There was none. The chute was smooth as polished marble.

No, not quite that smooth. This was sandstone, soft and porous, not marble, and between it and my wet body and wet clothing a certain friction was created. In addition, the stick had enabled me to reach a higher section of the S-curved chute, where the angle was more favorable. I discovered that I could move upward, inch by inch, through adhesion and with the help of the leveling tendency of the curve. I gave an extra little push with my big toe—the stones collapsed below, the stick clattered down—and crawled rather like a snail or slug, oozing slime, up over the rounded summit of the slide.

The next obstacle, the overhanging spout twelve feet above a deep plunge pool, looked impossible. It *was* impossible, but with the blind faith of despair I slogged into the water and swam underneath the drop-off and floundered about for a while, scrabbling at the slippery rock until my nerves and tiring muscles convinced by numbed brain that *this* was not the way. I swam back to solid ground and lay down to rest and die in comfort.

Far above I could see the sky, an irregular strip of blue between the dark, hard-edged canyon walls that seemed to lean toward each other as they towered above me. Across that narrow opening a small white cloud was passing, so lovely and precious and delicate and forever inaccessible that it broke the heart and made me weep like a woman, like a child. In all my life I had never seen anything so beautiful. But tears did not help. I shut them off, after a few minutes, and studied my problem.

The walls that rose on either side of the drop-off were literally perpendicular. Eroded by weathering, however, and not by the corrosion of rushing floodwater, they had a rough surface, chipped, broken, cracked. Where the walls joined the face of the overhang they formed almost a square corner, with a number of minute crevices and inch-wide shelves on either side. It might, after all, be possible. What did I have to lose?

When I had regained some measure of nerve and steadiness I got up off my back and tried the wall beside the pond, clinging to the rock with bare toes and fingertips and inching my way crabwise toward the corner. The watersoaked, heavy boots dangling from my neck, swinging back and forth with my every movement, threw me off balance and I fell into the pool. I swam out to the bank, unslung the boots and threw them up over the drop-off, out of sight. They'd be there if I ever needed them again.

Once more I attached myself to the wall, tenderly, sensitively, like a limpet, and very slowly, very cautiously, worked my way into the corner. Here I was able to climb upward, a few centimeters at a time, by bracing myself against the opposite sides and finding sufficient niches for fingers and toes. As I neared the top and the overhang became noticeable I prepared for a slip, planning to push myself away from the rock so as to fall into the center of the pool where the water was deepest. But it wasn't necessary. Somehow, with a skill and tenacity I could never have found in myself under ordinary circumstances, I managed to creep straight up that gloomy cliff and over the brink of the drop-off and into the flower of safety. My boots were floating under the surface of the little puddle above. As I poured the stinking water out of them and pulled them on and laced them up I discovered myself bawling again for the third time in three hours, the hot delicious tears of victory. And up above the clouds replied, with peals of thunder.

I emerged from that treacherous little canyon at sundown, with an enormous fire in the western sky and lightning overhead. Through sweet twilight and the sudden dazzling flare of lightning I hiked back along the Tonto Bench, bellowing the *Ode to Joy*. Long before I reached the place where I could descend safely to the main canyon and my camp, however, darkness set in, the clouds opened their bays and the rain poured down. I took shelter under a ledge in a shallow cave about three feet high—hardly room to sit up in. Others had been here before: the dusty floor of the little hole was littered with the droppings of birds, rats, jackrabbits and coyotes. There were also a few long gray pieces of scat with a curious twist at one tip—cougar? I didn't care. I had some matches with me, sealed in paraffin (the prudent explorer); I scraped together the handiest twigs and animal droppings and built a little fire and waited for the rain to stop.

It didn't stop. The rain came down for hours in alternate waves of storm and drizzle and I very soon had burnt up all the fuel within reach. No matter. I stretched out in the coyote den, pillowed my head on my arm and suffered through the long night, wet, cold, aching, hungry, dreaming claustrophobic nightmares. It was, all the same, one of the happiest nights of my life.

DIFFERENTIAL GEOGRAPHIES

Naming the land is a primal human response to the environment, and most places bear many names. A subtle theme in this passage from Charles McNichols's 1944 novel Crazy Weather, *set along the lower Colorado at the beginning of the twentieth century, is how our geographies can conflict: Havek's come from his ancestral "songlines"; South Boy's derive from his school textbook; and the Mormonhater's arise from wishful thinking.*

The moon came up over Arizona mountains, fifteen miles across the mesa—very red, very large, very bright. The little greasewoods cast long, pale, spindling shadows towards the now distant river. The breeze began blowing stronger. It was still hot, but the breeze made it pleasant.

Havek's song grew a little monotonous. The Raven brothers went name-traveling after they left the Sacred House. Havek's song became an unending recital of the names of mountains, canyons, springs, and streams that they saw as they wandered west to the San Bernardino Mountains where they looked upon the distant sea, then south and east to the mouth of the Colorado and east and north through Pima and Apache country.

An easy way to get your geography, if you could dream all that. Suppose I could go to sleep and dream the whole of Tarr and McMurry's [textbook of advanced geography] . . . South Boy was thinking when he saw the lights of Fort Mojave over to the left, where the mesa pushed a projecting peninsula right down to the river.

The Fort looked like a city to South Boy, with its dozen big buildings, two of them monsters—two stories high. There were very few lights tonight. He had seen it one night last winter, when school was in session— lights blazing from every window. A stupendous sight. Breath-taking. Counting the Indian children there were three hundred people in those buildings! Even now when there was only maintenance staff and a half-dozen lighted windows, the sight of the Fort was thrilling enough to make him forget the glory of the night and his haphazard speculations on dream singing.

A little farther north was a row of three lights close together—the trader's store. From there came the faint screech of a phonograph playing that new song "Redwing." He was too far away to see, but he knew the phonograph would be on a cracker box just outside the door. Young Mojaves would be perched in a long row on the hitching rail; old people, sitting on the ground; a white man or two from the Fort; maybe even a white lady sitting in the trader's rocking chair.

Havek stopped singing to listen. South Boy wished he would turn aside, but he went trotting on.

Suddenly the phonograph was drowned out by a chorus of strong voices.

"Oh the moon shines bright on pretty Redwing,
The breezes sighing, the night bird crying,
For beneath his star her brave is sleeping,
While Redwing's weeping
Her heart away."

Havek threw back his head and joined in with the distant singers. Nothing could be more different from the Raven singing than this tin-pan-alley product. But Havek proved the saying, "A Mojave can sing anything."

South Boy just listened with throbbing pleasure and a little melancholy, partly because of the sad plight of Redwing and partly because he had long since learned he could not sing.

The song faded, the lights grew dim and mingled with the lower stars. Before long they came to the place where the mesa dropped off again. Below them the mesquite floor stretched north as far as their eyes could see. Here and there were barren, alkali-encrusted playas that shone pale silver in the moonlight. A narrow, snaky lagoon began a mile away and wiggled off into the distance, its gray water showing a darker silver. There was a faint flicker of fire at the near end of it.

By that fire the hota would be holding the sing.

Havek stopped and leaned on his bow. South Boy stopped and looked at him expectantly. Havek spat into the dark shadow that fringed the edge of the cliff.

"Nebethee's down there, if he came up-river tonight."

"Uh-huh," said South Boy, speculatively. He walked to the very edge of the cliff and spat reflectively into the void, peering into the depth of the shadow, not anxiously, but with a certain sharp interest.

"Nebethee caught Pahto-shali-la and ate him, bones and all, and Pahto-shali-la was a full-sized man and a good fighter."

South Boy could have given Havek an argument on that. White people maintained that the Mojave got drunk and fell into the river at flood time. But South Boy's mind was too busy for arguments. He was swiftly reviewing the Mormonhater's ideas on the cannibalistic monster that the white people called the "Mojaves' devil."

"Are you afraid to go down there?" asked Havek.

South Boy shook his head. The time had been when he would have cringed with terror at the mention of Nebethee's name. When he was very small a big Indian girl had taken him to the brink of an old well and made him look down into the dark at their mingled reflections on the water. "Nebethee!" she said. "He will eat you!" That had scared him into a fit.

He was still too young to know better than to take tales of Indian doings to his mother—so he ran bellowing to her and had his first impression of Nebethee pretty well shaken out of him. Nebethee was just heathen nonsense. It was wicked to be afraid of him, because he was a heathen lie. By way of comfort he received the first of several lectures on the *real* or Presbyterian devil. A very different creature, indeed. South Boy had since acquired a shadowy, uneasy understanding of a complex of white or Christian devils that had overshadowed Nebethee completely.

But all that was by the way. About two years ago he had discovered by chance that in the dark of the moon the Mormonhater was doing some very mysterious hunting in the darkest places, and a good deal of it was around the big rock in the river below Needles that the Mojaves called "Nebethee's house." It took a year of chance, infrequent visits with the old trapper to wheedle the reason out of him.

The Mormonhater had many years ago seen a stuffed gorilla in a dime museum in San Francisco, so badly moth-eaten that it was about to fall apart. The proprietor was very sad about its condition. He said he'd give a hundred dollars for a fresh one.

The Mormonhater returned to his boat, his dogs and his trap lines, and in due course he began to give ear to the Mojave stories and descriptions of Nebethee. Then all at once it came to him! Nebethee was nothing else than a great, nocturnal ape. He wrote to the keeper of the dime museum and asked him how much he'd give for such a creature—hide and carcass.

He got a letter back—he even let South Boy read it. There in black and white was the offer of one million dollars for any gorilla shot in the Colorado River valley, plus an invitation for the Mormonhater to head a parade along the whole length of Market Street in an open carriage with the mayor of the city on one side of him, the carcass of the beast on the other.

The Mormonhater had fished his Bible out of his cartridge bag and made South Boy swear, with his right hand on the Book, that he'd never tell anyone.

South Boy went home and carefully read everything that the Advanced Geography had to say about the great apes, and studied the very inadequate picture shown in it.

He hadn't promised not to hunt the creature himself.

However, Nebethee-hunting had proven very poor around the ranch. Up here, down in that shadow, might be his golden opportunity.

A million dollars . . . that was all the money in the world. He'd give the Mormonhater half. He'd even let the Mormonhater share the carriage with him and the mayor and the late Nebethee.

Of course the geography said that gorillas were only found in Africa, and that they were herbivorous. But the geography said nothing at all about Mojaves or the Colorado River valley. It showed complete ignorance about this part of the world.

So South Boy stared eagerly into the cliff's shadow and started off in a trot along its rim, looking for a place to descend. While the idea of crowds of strange people gave him shudders under most conditions, the thought of that crowd along Market Street in San Francisco made him feel good. Maybe it was because they would be cheering him. That's what the Mormonhater said: "They'll be yelling their heads off!"

Not far away he found a slide: a place where the smaller boys from the Fort came on Saturdays to slide down the steep, gravelly face of the mesa on boards—the equivalent of tobogganing in a snowless country. He could go down there without getting his pants full of prickly pear and cholla.

So he paused at the top of the slide and called to Havek: "Tell me, have I heard truly? Does Nebethee look like a big, thick, hairy man that's hunchbacked and stooped over?"

"Truly! Truly!" said Havek, his breath whistling in his excitement.

A million dollars and a parade! thought South Boy as he disappeared into the black on a minor avalanche of gravel.

His hand was inside his shirt, gripping the butt of his short-gun. He had a feeling he'd be better satisfied if he had a weapon of heavier caliber—one that he'd tried out on something more than tin cans at very short range.

Still, this would be close-range work. He'd let Nebethee come twice arm-length and he'd put six bullets into his belly. After all, an ape was just a big, tough, hairy man. All the experts agreed—and there was hardly a man in the Valley but was at least a theoretical expert on homicide—that a bullet in the belly was the sure way of stopping a real tough man. The Foreman said (and it was well known he was more than a theoretical expert), "A bullet in the belly button beats two through the head."

The gravel stopped rolling under the seat of South Boy's pants and his feet hit soft dirt and hit running. He ran only as far as the first mesquite and there he crouched, his back protected by the thorny tree. He found he could see surprisingly well. There was nothing but low soap-weeds for yards around him. No hiding place for anything bigger than a rabbit. His heart beat hard, his imagination sent false, fleeting images to his eyes, but as a veteran of many a night hunt he knew he saw nothing real.

His heart eased and sank in slow, leaden disappointment.

He might have been there two minutes when he heard Havek's yell. The yell of a warrior who goes to look into the face of death. Havek was coming down the gravel slide, invisible, but audible.

Havek came running across the flat, a swiftly moving blackness in a world less black. Nothing else moved. South Boy, hope fading, got up and trotted after him, still crouching low, his hand on his belly-gun. Havek was out in the moonlight, and he stopped in a small white playa.

"South Boy!" he called anxiously. "South Boy!"

South Boy came walking out of the shadows, slowly. Somehow he'd been so sure of a million dollars and glory a minute ago. Now he had a sickening feeling.

That Mormonhater was crazy! Everyone said so. South Boy didn't want to believe it. The Mormonhater was his friend. But if Nebethee were an ape, there would have to be more than one. Apes have to breed and die like other creatures. Why hadn't he thought of that before working his hopes up so high?

He came up to where Havek stood, and walked by him in glum silence.

Havek was staring at him, his mouth open, the whites of his eyes showing. "Truly," he muttered. "Truly. A hawk-dreamer. His hands empty. He went down into Death's face. He walked slowly away. Truly—truly—truly—a Great Thing."

South Boy heard him and felt low and cheap. Havek thought he had done a brave thing. Instead he'd just made a fool of himself, believing a crazy man's story. He could not explain because he had promised the

Mormonhater. And how could he explain a thing like that to an Indian, anyway?

So he walked in silence, which was exactly what a Mojave would have done after an act of great courage. Havek followed him, murmuring delightedly; and South Boy felt all the more like a cheat, and his heart was lower than a snake's belly.

The trouble is, he was thinking, I act Indian one time and white another time and I get all mixed. He tried to think that idea out to make it more coherent, but he couldn't.

GARDEN IN THE SKY

Charles Lummis (1859–1928) was an early booster of the arid lands, a prolific author, and the founder of the Southwest Museum in Los Angeles. A born adventurer, he walked from his hometown of Chillicothe, Ohio, to Los Angeles during the fall of 1884 and early winter of 1885, a trip that would later lead to his celebrated—and not entirely truthful—book A Tramp Across the Continent (1892). The Arizona leg of his journey followed the wagon trail that later became Route 66; on later visits he took in the central and southern portions of the state.

Here, in a selection from Some Strange Corners of Our Country (1892), Lummis describes Tonto Natural Bridge (and its curious custodian). The bridge comprises six billion cubic yards of travertine so hard that, fortunately, no commercially practical way was ever found to quarry it. According to Apache legend, in ancient times a solid wall of stone formed the lower shore of a crystalline mountain lake in which a huge serpent dwelled. A great flood broke through the travertine embankment, leaving the arch in its wake, and the monster was washed down into the Salt River. Finding the waters too warm for its taste, the serpent made its way to the Gulf of California, where it presumably now dwells. In the summer of 1991, Tonto Natural Bridge became Arizona's twenty-sixth state park.

The Natural Bridge of Pine Creek, Arizona, is to the world's natural bridges what the Grand Cañon of the Colorado is to the world's chasms—the greatest, the grandest, the most bewildering. It is truly entitled to rank with the great natural wonders of the earth—as its baby brother in Virginia is not. Its grandeur is equally indescribable by artist and by writer—its vastness, and the peculiarities of its "architecture," make it one of the most difficult objects at which camera was ever leveled. No photograph can give more than a hint of its appalling majesty, no combination of photographs more than hints. There are photographs which do approximate justice to bits of the Grand Cañon, the Yosemite, the Yellowstone, the Redwoods, Niagara; there never will be of the Natural Bridge of Arizona—for reasons which you will understand later. But perhaps with words and pictures I can say enough to lead you some time to see for yourself this marvelous spot.

From Camp Verde the Natural Bridge lies a long, hard day's ride to the southeast. There is a government road—a very good one for that rough country—to Pine, so one may go by wagon all but five miles of the way. This road is fifteen miles longer to Pine than the rough and indistinct mail-trail of thirty-eight miles, which a stranger should not attempt to follow without a guide, and a weak traveler should not think of at all. About midway, this trail crosses the tremendous gorge of Fossil Creek—down and up pitches that try the best legs and lungs—and here is a very interesting spot. In the north side of Fossil Creek Cañon, close to the trail and in plain sight from it, are lonely little cave-houses that look down the sheer cliffs to the still pools below. Several miles down-stream there is a fort-house, also. Where the trail crosses the cañon there is no running water except in the rainy season; but a few hundred yards further down are the great springs. Like hundreds of other springs in the west, they are so impregnated with mineral that they are constantly building great round basins for themselves, and for a long distance flow down over bowl after bowl. But unlike other springs, those of Fossil Creek build their basins of what seems crude Mexican onyx. The fact that these waters quickly coat twigs or other articles with layers of this beautiful mineral gives rise to the name of Fossil—almost as odd a misnomer as has the "Petrified Spring" of which a New Mexico lady talks.

Passing through lonely Strawberry Valley, with its log farm-houses among prehistoric ruins, one comes presently over the last divide into the extreme western edge of the Tonto Basin, and down a steep cañon to the stiff little Mormon settlement of Pine, on the dry creek of the same name. From there to the Natural Bridge—five miles down-stream—there is no road at all, and the trail is very rough. But its reward waits at the end. Leaving the creek altogether and taking to the hills, we wind among the giant pines, then across a wild, lava-strewn mesa, and suddenly come upon the brink of a striking cañon fifteen hundred feet deep. Its west wall is an unspeakably savage jumble of red granite crags; the east side a wooded, but in most places impassably steep bluff. The creek has split through the ruddy granite to our right a wild, narrow portal, below which widens an almost circular little valley, half a mile across. Below this the cañon pinches again, and winds away by grim gorges to where the blue Mazatzals bar the horizon.

In the wee oasis at our feet there is as yet no sign of a natural bridge, nor of any other colossal wonder. There is a clearing amid the dense chaparral—a clearing with tiny house and barn, and rows of fruit trees, and fields of corn and alfalfa. They are thirteen hundred feet below us. Clambering down the steep and sinuous trail, among the chaparro and the huge flowering columns of the maguey, we come quite out of breath to the little cottage. It is a lovely spot, bowered in vines and flowers, with pretty walks and arbors by which ripples the clear brook from a big spring at the very door. A straight, thick-chested man, with twinkling eyes and long gray hair, is making sham battle with a big rooster, while a cat blinks at them from the bunk on the porch. These are the only inhabitants of this enchanted valley—old "Dave" Gowan, the hermit, and his two mateless pets. A quaint, sincere, large-hearted old man is he who has wrought this little paradise from utter wilderness by force of the ax. . . .

The old Scotchman is very taciturn at first, like all who have really learned the lessons of out-of-doors, but promptly accedes to a request to be shown his bridge. He leads the way out under his little bower of clematis, down the terraced vineyard, along the corn-field, and into the pretty young orchard of peach and apricot. Still no token of what we seek; and we begin to wonder if a bridge so easily hidden can be so very big after all. There is even no sign of a stream.

And on a sudden, between the very trees, we stand over a little water-worn hole and peer down into space. *We are on the bridge now! The orchard is on the bridge!* Do you know of any other fruit-trees that grow in so strange a garden? Of any other two-storied farm? The rock of the bridge is at this one point less than ten feet thick; and this odd little two-foot peep-hole, like a broken plank in the giant floor, was cut through by water.

"Wait," chuckles the hermit, his eyes twinkling at our wonder; "wait!" And he leads us a few rods onward, till we stand beside an old juniper on the very brink of a terrific gorge. We are upon the South Arch of the bridge, dizzily above the clear, noisy stream, looking down the savage cañon in whose wilds its silver thread is straightway lost to view. . . .

Circling south along the southeast "pier," we start down a rugged, difficult, and at times dangerous trail. A projecting crag of the pier—destined to be a great obstacle, later, in our photographic attempts—shuts the bridge from view till we near the bottom of the gorge, and then it bursts upon us in sudden wonder. The hand of man never reared such an arch, nor shall ever rear, as the patient springs have gnawed here from eternal rock. Dark and stern, and fairly crushing in its immensity, towers that terrific arch of rounded limestone. The gorge is wild beyond telling, choked with giant boulders and somber evergreens and bristling cacti until it comes to the very jaws of that grim gateway, and there even vegetation seems to shrink back in awe. Now one begins to appreciate the magnitude of the bridge, a part of whose top holds a five-acre orchard. In its eternal shadow is room for an army.

THE WESTERN DESERTS

"The desert is no lady," writes Chicana poet Pat Mora:

> She screams at the spring sky,
> dances with her skirts high,
> kicks sand, flings tumbleweed
> digs her nails into all flesh.

Martha Summerhayes (1846–1911) arrived in Arizona in 1874 with her husband, William Summerhayes, an officer attached to General George Crook's garrison for the Department of Arizona. They lived at Fort Apache at the height of the American government's quarter-century war against the Western Apache tribes and later were assigned to an infantry camp outside Ehrenberg, a thriving mining center and port on the lower Colorado River. Lieutenant Summerhayes assured his wife that the new post would be quite suitable, for she could board the steamship that came upriver from the Gulf of California every two weeks or so and travel on to San Francisco whenever the isolation became too much to bear.

In this passage from Vanished Arizona *(1908), an essential work of Southwestern literature, Martha Summerhayes recalls, three decades after the fact, the last stages of the hard wagon journey down from the highlands of the Apachería, through the canyonlands near Prescott, and on across the desolation to the river, where, she discovered, the desert is indeed no lady.*

At the end of a week, we started forth for Ehrenberg. Our escort was now sent back to Camp Apache, . . . so our outfit consisted of one ambulance and one army wagon. One or two soldiers went along, to help with the teams and the camp.

We travelled two days over a semi-civilized country, and found quite comfortable ranches where we spent the nights. The greatest luxury was fresh milk, and we enjoyed that at these ranches in Skull Valley. They kept American cows, and supplied Whipple Barracks with milk and butter. We drank, and drank, and drank again, and carried a jugful to our bedside. The third day brought us to Cullen's Ranch, at the edge of the desert. Mrs. Cullen was a Mexican woman and had a little boy named Daniel; she cooked us a delicious supper of stewed chicken, and fried eggs, and good bread, and then she put our boy to bed in Daniel's crib. I felt so grateful to her; and with a return of physical comfort, I began to think that life, after all, might be worth the living.

Hopefully and cheerfully the next morning we entered the vast Colorado desert. This was verily the desert, more like the desert which our imagination pictures, than the one we had crossed in September from [Camp] Mohave. It seemed so white, so bare, so endless, and so still; irreclaimable, eternal, like Death itself. The stillness was appalling. We saw great numbers of lizards darting about like lightning; they were nearly as white as the sand itself, and sat up on their hind legs and looked at us with their pretty, beady black eyes. It seemed very far off from everywhere and everybody, this desert—but I knew there was a camp somewhere awaiting us, and our mules trotted patiently on. Towards noon they began to raise their heads and sniff the air; they knew that water was near. They quickened their pace, and we soon drew up before a large wooden structure. There were no trees nor grass around it. A Mexican worked the machinery with the aid of a mule, and water was bought for our twelve animals, at so much per head. The place was called Mesquite Wells; the man dwelt alone in his desolation, with no living being except his mule for company. How could he endure it! I was not able, even faintly, to comprehend it; I had not lived long enough. He occupied a small hut, and there he stayed, year in and year out, selling water to the passing traveller; and I fancy that travellers were not so frequent at Mesquite Wells a quarter of a century ago.

The thought of that hermit and his dreary surroundings filled my mind for a long time after we drove away, and it was only when we halted and a soldier got down to kill a great rattlesnake near the ambulance, that my thoughts were diverted. The man brought the rattles to us and the new toy served to amuse my little son.

At night we arrived at Desert Station [fifteen miles west of present Vicksburg Junction]. There was a good ranch there, kept by Hunt and Dudley, Englishmen, I believe. I did not see them, but I wondered who they were and why they stayed in such a place. They were absent at the time; perhaps they had mines or something of the sort to look after. One is always imagining things about people who live in such extraordinary places. At all events, whatever Messrs. Hunt and Dudley were doing down there, their ranch was clean and attractive, which was more than could be said of the place where we stopped the next night, a place called Tyson's

Wells.[1] We slept in our tent that night, for of all places on the earth a poorly kept ranch in Arizona is the most melancholy and uninviting. It reeks of everything unclean, morally and physically. . . .

One more day's travel across the desert brought us to our El Dorado.

A close look at a few plants can tell us much about the whole of a lifezone. In this passage from Tom Miller's collection Arizona: The Land and the People, *biologist and river runner Larry Stevens describes a few characteristic plants of the Mojave Desert, notably the rare, strangely beautiful Joshua tree. The Mojave differs from Arizona's other deserts chiefly in that it receives most of its scant rainfall in the winter.*

Near Oatman, one sees brittlebush, teddybear cholla, and Mojave yucca. Brittlebush, among the hardiest of the low desert plants, puts out a banquet of yellow, daisy-like flowers in March and April, and in good years turns the Mojave's piedmont and alluvial fans to gold. Most of the desert year, however, it stands, stubbornly resisting the heat, its grey-green, finely haired leaves shimmering in the desert sun. The plant is well adapted to desert conditions; but if the summer rains fail, its beautiful foliage gradually withers and drops to the ground, and the plant appears dead. These exceptional plants produce a toxin which leaches from fallen leaves and prevents other species of plants from germinating beneath the brittlebush's low canopy, where they might preempt light, water, and soil nutrients.

The Mojave yucca is a sturdy relative of the Joshua tree. It forms a short, stout trunk and points a nest of sword-like leaves skyward. To say this species is "well-defended" is a gross understatement, and one can only

1. Tyson's Wells was renamed Quartzsite in 1893 with the establishment of the post office. The desert hamlet is famous for its having been a haunt of Hadj Ali, who arrived in 1859 to tend to the herd of camels that Lieutenant William Beale had urged be imported for service in the desert cavalry. His name quickly anglicized to "Hi Jolly," Ali later became a prospector and merchant. He died at Quartzsite in 1903, and a monument was later erected there in his honor.

wonder what Cenozoic beasts so preferred Mojave yucca pods that the plant was forced to these extremes of self-defense.

In the shade of creosotebushes and yuccas, zebra-tailed lizards can be found. The zebra-tailed lizard is a diurnal insectivore which wags its black-and-white-striped tail and thermoregulates by sunning or shading beneath creosotebush and bursage. One of the fastest North American lizards, it has been clocked at speeds of nearly twenty miles per hour. It feeds on insects, including the golden fruit flies that plague desert visitors.

The Joshua tree, named by early Mormons, is the largest and most characteristic plant endemic to the Mojave Desert and perhaps best expresses the unique spirit of the region. It is in the genus *Yucca* and has been given the Latin species designation of *brevifolia* for its short, dagger-like leaves. It forms a branching tree thirty to forty feet high and bears stalks of big, succulent, creamy white flowers in the spring. These flowers produce a musty odor and bloom for a single night.

The successful establishment of a Joshua tree seedling is a rare event. Joshua trees have somewhat circumvented the problems associated with germination in a hostile environment by sending out running shoots that sprout up some distance away from the parent tree. The yucca skipper takes advantage of this root-sprouting strategy. It is somehow able to distinguish the preferred runner-sprouted Joshua trees from seedling trees, and lays eggs on them. The larvae hatch, drop to the ground, and burrow into the running roots to feed on the dense tissue there.

An essential problem with our understanding of the evolution of a species such as the Joshua tree is our lack of appreciation of time. We tend to regard present species as having evolved in conditions similar to what we experience in our brief lives. But many present-day Mojave species survived drastic climatic changes in the late Pleistocene, having evolved much earlier and under more rigorous conditions. We tend to ignore the fact that the plants and animals of our American deserts evolved alongside the important megafaunal grazers, browsers, and carnivores which have only recently died out. The influence these animals, especially the herbivores, exerted on our modern plants may be reflected today in strange patterns of plant growth and distribution.

Joshua trees, for example, do not often occur in valleys which seem suitable for them. Mammoths and giant ground sloths almost certainly relished Joshua tree pods. A fair amount of ground sloth dung containing Joshua tree remains has been found. The seeds of this strange tree are hard and black and probably passed safely through the guts of these great beasts, as juniper and mesquite seeds do through cattle today. Certainly coyotes, rodents, and birds may now disperse some of these seeds, but germination is a rare event, and tens of thousands or even millions of seeds need to be produced and scattered before even a single tree will germinate successfully.

Yet germinate they do, and around them in the Joshua tree forest of the Mojave Desert teems an abundance of life. Clumsy Gila monsters, mildly venomous black and orange lizards, feed on birds' eggs and young rodents. Red-tailed hawks nest in Joshua trees and prey on rabbits, ground squirrels, and snakes. Found almost solely beneath fallen Joshua trees, the reclusive desert night lizard feeds on termites in the rotting logs. Rattlesnakes, jackrabbits, coyotes, cactus wrens, scorpions, and ravens—the diversity of life in the Joshua tree forest is astonishing.

The real spirit of this desert world is in the sun-baked ground and in the strange plants and creatures that hail from it. The mystery may be too large and simple for any of us to ever fully appreciate, especially in the Mojave, where Nature plays her cards close to the vest, like the gambler she is.

The rugged country between Yuma and Gila City—a stagecoach stop some twenty-five miles to the east that J. Ross Browne said "consisted of three chimneys and a coyote," and that has since been swallowed by the desert— is difficult enough for modern travelers. In the nineteenth century, it was nearly impassable without considerable teeth-chattering, as Richard Hinton, the author of the Hand-Book to Arizona, *discovered, much to his discomfort. Still, he found much to admire in the passing landscape, all the while pondering how best to alter what he saw.*

Of one thing heed must be taken. In no place is the spirit of courtesy and mutual accommodation more needed than in a crowded stage-coach starting out on a long journey. Rolling day and night over gravelly mesa, sandy river road, and stony mountain pass, there will be ample room for the exercise of all the finer courtesies and social amenities. The aspect of much of the scenery along this gray valley road, bleak, rocky mesa track, lined on either side by volcanic ranges of jagged peaks and serrated slopes, so brown and sere, and with not a growing thing to relieve the barrenness of their sides, is not of a character to be desired for a steady landscape. But it has its own beauty—rare, because it is so different from what one sees elsewhere—and possessing charms that are all its own, unique and captivating. The graceful mesquite and malverde trees grow everywhere, and the numberless varieties of the cactus make the scene still stranger to an unaccustomed vision.

The first stage out is to Gila city. This now consists of a comfortable stage station, a broad expanse of tillable valley land, sometimes overflowed by the river, which is at times "mighty uncertain," and a steep range of volcanic hills coming close to the highways—is for a dozen miles or so hot, heavy and sandy. It is hardly fair to say sandy, as it is really a friable alluvial loam of grayish hue and loose texture. Several ranches are passed, showing that the Gila bottom is cultivable. With irrigation every square mile of the Gila valley is capable of producing prolific crops of grains and semi-tropical fruits, as well as cotton and sugar in great abundance. The river is able to furnish all the water needed, and a good deal more. It would take no very great skill in engineering, and not a very large sum of money either, to construct reservoirs or lakes in which to receive and store the overflow. There are natural basins or dry lakes into which, by simple means, the water could be conveyed. An atmosphere of wonderful richness and brilliance covers the scene like a gorgeous canopy of prismatic colors, and the vision is lost in the immensity of the distances.

THINKING LIKE A MOUNTAIN

❖

The work of wildlife biologist Aldo Leopold (1887–1948) has informed that of almost every environmental and nature writer who has followed. In the early years of the twentieth century, he served as a game manager in the mountains of eastern Arizona near the New Mexico border and the present-day White Mountain Apache Nation, in what many people regard as the most beautiful part of the state. Although modern highways lace the high plateau and the logging industry is everywhere present, the area remains ruggedly wild, with lightning-rent pine trees, black bears, rattlesnakes, and trout splashing in the clear waters of the Blue River.

The railroad towns to which Leopold refers in this passage from his classic Sand County Almanac *(1949) are Holbrook and Winslow, respectively some sixty and eighty miles—or two days' ride—northwest of the White Mountains.*

When I first lived in Arizona, the White Mountain was a horseman's world. Except along a few main routes, it was too rough for wagons. There were no cars. It was too big for foot travel; even sheepherders rode. Thus by elimination, the county-sized plateau known as "on top" was the exclusive domain of the mounted man: mounted cowman, mounted sheepman, mounted forest officer, mounted trapper, and those unclassified mounted men of unknown origin and uncertain destination always found on frontiers. It is difficult for this generation to understand this aristocracy of space based upon transport.

No such thing existed in the railroad towns two days to the north, where you had your choice of travel by shoe leather, burro, cowhorse, buckboard, freight wagon, caboose, or Pullman. Each of these modes of movement corresponded to a social caste, the members of which spoke a distinctive vernacular, wore distinctive clothes, ate distinctive food, and patronized different saloons. Their only common denominator was a democracy of debt to the general store, and a communal wealth of Arizona dust and Arizona sunshine.

As one proceeded southward across the plains and mesas toward the White Mountain, these castes dropped out one by one as their respective modes of travel became impossible, until finally, "on top," the horseman ruled the world.

Henry Ford's revolution has of course abolished all this. Today the plane has given even the sky to Tom, Dick, and Harry.

In winter the top of the mountain was denied even to horsemen, for the snow piled deep on the high meadows, and the little canyons up which the only trails ascended drifted full to the brim. In May every canyon roared with an icy torrent, but soon thereafter you could "top out"—if your horse had the heart to climb half a day through knee-deep mud.

In the little village at the foot of the mountain there existed, each spring, a tacit competition to be the first rider to invade the high solitudes. Many of us tried it, for reasons we did not stop to analyze. Rumor ran fast. Whoever did it first wore a kind of horseman's halo. He was "man-of-the-year."

The mountain spring, storybooks to the contrary notwithstanding, did not come with a rush. Balmy days alternated with bitter winds, even after the sheep had gone up. I have seen few colder nights than a drab gray mountain meadow, sprinkled with complaining ewes and half-frozen lambs, pelted by hail and snow. Even the gay nutcrackers humped their backs to these spring storms.

The mountain in summer had as many moods as there were days and weathers; the dullest rider, as well as his horse, felt these moods to the marrow of his bones.

On a fair morning the mountain invited you to get down and roll in its new grass and flowers (your less inhibited horse did just this if you failed to keep a tight rein). Every living thing sang, chirped, and burgeoned. Massive pines and firs, storm-tossed these many months, soaked up the sun in towering dignity. Tassel-eared squirrels, poker-faced but exuding emotion with voice and tail, told you insistently what you already knew full well: that never had there been so rare a day, or so rich a solitude to spend it in.

An hour later, thunderheads may have blotted out the sun, while your erstwhile paradise cowered under the impending lash of lightning, rain, and hail. Black gloom hung poised, as over a bomb with the fuse lighted. Your horse jumped at every rolling pebble, every crackling twig. When you turned in the saddle to unlash your slicker, he shied, snorted, and trembled as if you were about to unfurl the scroll of an Apocalypse. When

I hear anyone say he does not fear lightning, I still remark inwardly: he has never ridden The Mountain in July.

The explosions are fearsome enough, but more so are the smoking slivers of stone that sing past your ear when the bolt crashes into a rimrock. Still more so are the splinters that fly when a bolt explodes a pine. I remember one gleaming white one, 15 feet long, that stabbed deep into the earth at my feet and stood there humming like a tuning fork.

It must be poor life that achieves freedom from fear.

The top of the mountain was a great meadow, half a day's ride across, but do not picture it as a single amphitheater of grass, hedged in by a wall of pines. The edges of that meadow were scrolled, curled, and crenulated with an infinity of bays and coves, points and stringers, peninsulas and parks, each one of which differed from all the rest. No man knew them all, and every day's ride offered a gambler's chance of finding a new one. I say "new" because one often had the feeling, riding into some flower-spangled cove, that if anyone had ever been here before, he must of necessity have sung a song, or written a poem.

This feeling of having this day discovered the incredible accounts, perhaps, for the profusion of initials, dates, and cattle brands inscribed on the patient bark of aspens at every mountain camp site. In these inscriptions one could, in any day, read the history of *Homo texanus* and his culture, not in the cold categories of anthropology, but in terms of the individual career of some founding father whose initials you recognized as the man whose son bested you at horse-trading, or whose daughter you once danced with. Here, dated in the 'nineties, was his simple initial, without brand, inscribed no doubt when he first arrived alone on the mountain as an itinerant cowpuncher. Next, a decade later, his initial plus brand; by that time he had become a solid citizen with an "outfit," acquired by thrift, natural increase, and perhaps a nimble rope. Next, only a few years old, you found his daughter's initial, inscribed by some enamored youth aspiring not only to the lady's hand, but to the economic succession.

The old man was dead now; in his later years his heart had thrilled only to his bank account and to the tally of his flocks and herds, but the aspen revealed that in his youth he too had felt the glory of the mountain spring.

The history of the mountain was written not only in aspen bark, but in its place names. Cow-country place names are lewd, humorous, ironic, or sentimental, but seldom trite. Usually they are subtle enough to draw inquiry from new arrivals, whereby hangs that web of tales which, full spun, constitutes the local folk-lore.

For example, there was "The Boneyard," a lovely meadow where bluebells arched over the half-buried skulls and scattered vertebrae of cows long since dead. Here in the 1880s a foolish cowman, newly arrived from the warm valleys of Texas, had trusted the allurements of the mountain summer and essayed to winter his herd on mountain hay. When the November storms hit, he and his horse had floundered out, but not his cows.

Again, there was "The Campbell Blue," a headwater of the Blue River to which an early cowman had brought himself a bride. The lady, tiring of rocks and trees, had yearned for a piano. A piano was duly fetched, a Campbell piano. There was only one mule in the county capable of packing it, and only one packer capable of the almost superhuman task of balancing such a load. But the piano failed to bring contentment; the lady decamped; and when the story was told me, the ranch cabin was already a ruin of sagging logs.

Again there was "Frijole Cienega," a marshy meadow walled in by pines, under which stood, in my day, a small log cabin used by any passer-by as an overnight camp. It was the unwritten law for the owner of such real estate to leave flour, lard, and beans, and for the passer-by to replenish such stock as he could. But one luckless traveler, trapped there for a week by storms, had found only beans. This breach of hospitality was sufficiently notable to be handed down to history as a place name.

Finally, there was "Paradise Ranch," an obvious platitude when read from a map, but something quite different when you arrived there at the end of a hard ride. It lay tucked away on the far side of a high peak, as any proper paradise should. Through its verdant meadows meandered a singing trout stream. A horse left for a month on this meadow waxed so fat that rain-water gathered in a pool on his back. After my first visit to Paradise Ranch I remarked to myself: what else *could* you call it?

Despite several opportunities to do so, I have never returned to the White Mountain. I prefer not to see what tourists, roads, sawmills, and logging railroads have done for it, or to it. I hear young people, not yet born when I first rode out "on top," exclaim about it as a wonderful place. To this, with an unspoken mental reservation, I agree.

✛

Joseph Garrison Pearce (1874–1958) had the distinction of being Arizona's first United States forest ranger, headquartered in the alpine country near Nutrioso, where he had grown up. Pearce patrolled a huge expanse of mountains, the same territory that Aldo Leopold came to know so well a few years later, and wrote of his adventures on the Mogollon Rim in unpublished memoirs now housed at the Arizona Historical Society.

The Black Mesa Forest Reservation included the White and the Blue mountains, country almost unknown to the white man, range on range and ridge on ridge of thick close-standing pine and blue spruce and wide groves of white aspen, interrupted by clearings in the valleys where no trees grew. There were very few trails. Some of the timber was thicker than a jungle to get through.

The forest was alive with game. . . . The streams ran full of trout, with not enough fishermen to keep them caught out. When I was a boy, the turkey came down within a mile of our ranch at Taylor, and we could hear them gobbling in the spring. But as the country settled up, they moved back into the mountains. The forest was thick with deer, every kind, black-tail, mule, white-tail. And I couldn't ride a day in the forest without seeing a flock of antelope streak over the hills and into the canyons, their white rumps bouncing. Mountain lions had their hide-outs deep in the forest, and from their caves sneaked out into civilized country to prey on sheep and newborn calves. Sometimes I spotted mountain sheep high on the ridges. . . .

I got well acquainted with those mountains, living there for three years alone and during the fire season on the move all the time. I've often been lost in a storm. There are two kinds of lost: being turned around and being stranded. For being turned around there's one way to safety that I've never known to fail. A good horse—not a bronc, mind you—but a good saddle horse will always remember the last place where he has had feed and water, and he will know the way there, give him his head. In a storm if I've thought the horse could make it and I could stand the severe cold, and my *cabeza* was twisted about where I was, I'd just say, "Come on, Bob. Let's go home." A man never needs to be lost riding a gentle horse.

Storm stranded is another matter. I've been in snow so thick with whirlwinds in those mountains I couldn't see ten feet in front of my nose, and blizzards howling for three days without let-up. In a storm like that there's no use trying to go on; you have to make some kind of shelter for yourself. A hatchet was always part of my equipment.

I'd unload my pack horse and unsaddle my horse and leave the stock to shift for themselves. Then I'd stretch my rope from one pine to another, cut branches from the small pines and lean them slantwise on each side of the rope. When I was done, there was a cozy shelter. Next I'd collect dry wood—and a forest man can always find it—and pile the wood inside, build me a fire. There I'd lie snug with my fire and wait for the storm to run itself down.

When [U.S. Forest Service director Gifford] Pinchot came for his inspection of the Black Mesa Forest, I took him along a trail I'd blazed some time before beyond Alpine southward toward Clifton. We came to the place the Blue Range breaks off almost sheer, and down below the mountains roll away toward Clifton.

Pinchot said: "Guess we'll have to turn around and go back. We can't get down off this mountain, Joe."

Then I told him I'd blazed the trail down there so that a rider could get through to Clifton. To prove it, we went down, leading our horses.

That evening in camp I asked him: "Do you think there'll ever be a wagon road there, down the Blue Range to the flats?"

He got a laugh out of that. "There'll never even be a good horse trail," he said. "The only way a man'll ever get down there easily is to grow wings and fly down."

That was forty years ago. And now every day automobiles go along through there and roll down the slopes of the Blue Range following almost exact the trail I blazed in 1899, now the Coronado Trail.

Paula Castillo, the mother of Yaqui deer singer Felipe Molina, tells how the mountains were created in a story combining Yaqui belief with Spanish Catholicism.

When Our Mother Mary and Jesus lived on Earth in the present day Yaqui country the wilderness was without mountains. One day Jesus got mad at

Our Mother for some reason. Jesus told Our Mother that he was going to leave home. Our Mother tried to discourage him from leaving. His mind was already set on going so he readied himself for the departure into the wilderness. Our Mother prepared her son some lunch, which was *sak tusi* (cornmeal). Our Mother put the *sak tusi* in a new clean cloth and tied it into a bundle on a stick so that Jesus could carry it on his shoulders.

Jesus left on his journey and wandered in the wilderness. For many days he traveled in the wilderness and his cloth bundle began to tear. From this small tear the *sak tusi* began to spill out onto the ground. So all the *sak tusi* that fell to the ground at that time are now the mountains we see today.

ROAD FEVER

Wallace Stegner has observed that "western literature . . . has been largely a literature not of place but of motion." As if determined to prove him right, from 1946 to 1950 the Beat Generation chronicler and patron saint Jack Kerouac (1922–1969) wandered the endless highways of America in the company of his friend Neal Cassady, later a principal character in Tom Wolfe's Electric Kool-Aid Acid Test. *From 1948 to 1957 Kerouac wrote and rewrote his most famous book, a barely fictionalized account of his travels called* On the Road. *(A media myth, which he did nothing to discourage, had it that Kerouac wrote his fast-paced book in three weeks on a steady diet of Benzedrine.) The book made him justly famous, but Kerouac never recaptured its narrative heights.*

On the third of his four-leg transcontinental marathons, in the winter of 1949, Kerouac came to Tucson by way of U.S. 80 in the company of Cassady (called, in the novel, Dean Moriarty), Cassady's girlfriend Marylou, and a one-armed hitchhiker named Alfred. There they spent two days visiting the writer Alan Harrington—here named Hal Hingham—who had left a corporate job in New York to write his novel The Revelations of Dr. Modesto *(1955). Harrington lived at the home of his mother, anthropologist Gwyneth Harrington Xavier, who had some years earlier married the Tohono O'odham shaman and leader Juan Xavier.*

We passed Las Cruces, New Mexico, in the night and arrived in Arizona at dawn. I woke from a deep sleep to find everybody sleeping like lambs and the car parked God knows where, because I couldn't see out the steamy windows. I got out of the car. We were in the mountains: there was a heaven of sunrise, cool purple airs, red mountainsides, emerald pastures in valleys, dew, and transmuting clouds of gold; on the ground gopher holes, cactus, mesquite. It was time for me to drive on. I pushed Dean and the kid over and went down the mountain with the clutch in and the motor off to save gas. In this manner I rolled into Benson, Arizona. It occurred to me that I had a pocket watch Rocco had just given me for a birthday present, a four-dollar watch. At the gas station I asked the man if he knew a pawnshop in Benson. It was right next door to the station. I knocked, someone got up out of bed, and in a minute I had a dollar for the watch. It went into the tank. Now we had enough gas for Tucson. But suddenly a big pistol-packing trooper appeared, just as I was ready to pull out, and asked to see my driver's license. "The fella in the back seat has the license," I said. Dean and Marylou were sleeping together under the blanket. The cop told Dean to come out. Suddenly he whipped out his gun and yelled, "Keep your hands up!"

"Offisah," I heard Dean say in the most unctious and ridiculous tones, "offisah, I was only buttoning my flah." Even the cop almost smiled. Dean came out, muddy, ragged, T-shirted, rubbing his belly, cursing, looking everywhere for his license and his car papers. The cop rummaged through our back trunk. All the papers were straight.

"Only checking up," he said with a broad smile. "You can go on now. Benson ain't a bad town actually; you might enjoy it if you had breakfast here."

"Yes yes yes," said Dean, paying absolutely no attention to him, and drove off. We all sighed with relief. The police are suspicious when gangs of youngsters come by in new cars without a cent in their pockets and have to pawn watches. "Oh, they're always interfering," said Dean, "but he was a much better cop than that rat in Virginia. They try to make headline arrests; they think every car going by is some big Chicago gang. They ain't got nothin else to do." We drove on to Tucson.

Tucson is situated in beautiful mesquite riverbed country, overlooked by the snowy Catalina range. The city was one big construction job; the people transient, wild, ambitious, busy, gay; washlines, trailers; bustling downtown streets with banners; altogether very Californian. Fort Lowell Road, out where Hingham lived, wound along lovely riverbed trees in the flat desert. We saw Hingham himself brooding in the yard. He was a writer; he had come to Arizona to work on his book in peace. He was a tall, gangly, shy satirist who mumbled to you with his head turned away and always said funny things. His wife and baby were with him in the dobe [*sic*] house, a small one that his Indian stepfather had built. His mother lived across the yard in her own house. She was an excited American woman who loved pottery, beads, and books. Hingham had heard of Dean through letters from New York. We came down on him like a cloud, every one of us hungry, even Alfred, the crippled hitchhiker. Hingham was wearing an old sweater and smoking a pipe in the keen desert air. His mother came out and invited us into her kitchen to eat. We cooked noodles in a great pot.

Then we all drove to a crossroads liquor store, where Hingham cashed a check for five dollars and handed me the money.

There was a brief good-by. "It certainly was pleasant," said Hingham, looking away. Beyond some trees, across the sand, a great neon sign of a roadhouse glowed red. Hingham always went there for a beer when he was tired of writing. He was very lonely, he wanted to get back to New York. It was sad to see his tall figure receding in the dark as we drove away, just like the other figures in New York and New Orleans: they stand uncertainly underneath immense skies, and everything about them is drowned. Where go? what do? what for?—sleep. But this foolish gang was bending onward.

A composition of the Globe Business and Professional Women's Club in commemoration of the statewide convention of such clubs held in Jerome in May 1927, this delightfully amateurish poem nicely captures the roller-coaster landscape and therefore the rollercoaster roads—of the Arizona interior. The "land of feud" refers to the so-called Pleasant Valley war of the 1870s, which took place in the highlands near Young.

We come from Globe, where the high pinals,
　　Look over and shelter our town,
Where the white of the snow, in the sun-set's glow,
　　Contrasts with the Oak Leaves, brown.

Past the Roosevelt Dam, blessed inland sea,
　　Right there, at Globe's front door,
With its wavelets of crystal silver,
　　And its flowerbordered shore.

Then up thru Tonto Basin,
　　Our motor goes throbbing, strong,
Thru that land of feud and mystery,
　　And of beautiful birds in song.

And on to the town of Payson,
  Midst the pines and cedars too,
And on thru the Strawberry valley,
  Neath skies of the deepest blue.

And on to that beautiful highway,
  That corkscrews its way on down,
Where FOSSIL CREEK, like a crooked stick,
  Flows on twixt its banks of brown.

And to your own loved country,
  No wonder you call it home,
For everything that's wonderful
  You have here in JEROME.

And the warmth of your hospitality,
  Is heralded afar.
We heard of it first from the sighing breeze,
  And again from a shooting star.

And again we'el say ere we go away,
  Before we start for home;
We're glad we're here; We love you dear;
  DEAR HOME LIKE, OLD JEROME.

Like many another Arizonan, Badger Clark (1883–1962) came to the Southwest for reasons of health, having contracted tropical fever while fighting in Cuba during the Spanish American War. He settled in Tombstone and became a rancher and developer. His Sun and Saddle Leather *(1915), a book of cowboy ballads from which this poem, "Ridin'," is taken, remains a staple of Southwestern Americana and is a fitting homage to the wagon trails that preceded modern highways.*

———————

There is some that like the city—
  Grass that's curried smooth and green,

Theaytres and stranglin' collars,
   Wagons run by gasoline—
But for me it's hawse and saddle
   Every day without a change,
And a desert sun a-blazin'
   On a hundred miles of range.

   Just a-ridin', a-ridin'—
     Desert ripplin' in the sun,
   Mountains blue along the skyline—
     I don't envy anyone
      When I'm ridin'.

When my feet is in the stirrups
   And my hawse is on the bust,
With his hooves a-flashin' lightnin'
   From a cloud of golden dust,
And the bawlin' of the cattle
   Is a-comin' down the wind,
Then a finer life than ridin'
   Would be mighty hard to find.

   Just a-ridin', a-ridin'—
     Splittin' long cracks through the air,
   Stirrin' up a baby cyclone,
     Rippin' up the prickly pear
      As I'm ridin'.

I don't need no art exhibits
   When the sunset does her best,
Paintin' everlastin' glory
   On the mountains to the west
And your opery looks foolish
   When the night-bird starts his tune
And the desert's silver mounted
   By the touches of the moon.

   Just a-ridin', a-ridin—
     Who kin envy kings and czars
   When the coyotes down the valley

Are a-singin' to the stars
  If he's ridin'?

When my earthly trail is ended
  And my final bacon curled
And the last great roundup's finished
  At the Home Ranch of the world,
I don't want no harps nor haloes
  Robes nor other dressed up things—
Let me ride the starry ranges
  On a pinto hawse with wings!

  Just a-ridin', a-ridin'—
    Nothin' I'd like half so well
  As a-roundin' up the sinners
    That have wandered out of Hell
    And a-ridin'.

STONE

The language of geology has a music of its own, as witness Scottish writer Hugh MacDiarmid's beautiful poem "On a Raised Beach" and this passage from Richard Hinton's Hand-Book to Arizona *(1879) describing the highlands of Yavapai County.*

In the vicinity of Prescott the general direction of the mountain ranges, quartz veins, and dikes trends from north-west to south-east. The country rocks are metamorphic slates, feldspathic granites of various tints, veins of epidote and hornblende, quartzites and white quartz stained with oxyd of iron. These last are very prominent, of great length and width, but rarely carry any precious metals. These veins are in most instances barely outcropping upon the tops of the rounded hills, but easily traced by the float. In some localities trap rocks and metamorphic slate dikes are very prominent. In the vicinity of the slate formations the principal metal-bearing veins are to be found, the metal veins usually running parallel, in a few instances only crossing at nearly right angles. Volcanic trap rock and scoria lie scattered over the table lands or mesas, disintegrated, then washed away, leaving the rounded foothills with their primitive characters but slightly disturbed. The alluvial detritus was washed into the valleys, impregnated with alkaline salts and vegetable matter, forming a dark, rich mold, and producing splendid crops. Gold has been found in nearly every locality in Yavapai county wherever diligent search has been made, both in veins and in bars and gulches. It is noticed that the lodes when first opened carry a good percentage of gold, but at a greater depth run into or carry a large per cent. of silver. It is found also in the granitic, feldspathic, quartzose, hornblendic, slate, and talcose rocks, free and intimately mixed with various sulphides, often in beautiful crystals of the octohedral form; wire gold has been found; also scales and nuggets of respectable size.

✢

John S. Griffin, medical officer on the Emory Boundary Expedition of 1848, gives this account of the petroglyphs called Painted Rocks, not far from Gila Bend and north of Interstate 8.

———————————

Nov. 17th & 18th. One days march on the River is so much like unto another that one description will do for all that is to say—sand, dust, & a black stone, so blistered from the effects of heat that they look like they had hardly got cool—no grass, nothing but weeds & cactus. The River here [near Dateland] is some 60 or 80 yards wide—on an average 3 feet deep and rapid. We have seen more water fowel in the last two days, than we have yet met with on the River—ducks, brant geese & swan. The cotton wood shows the effect of frost very little—not more than the same tree did when we left the Rio Grande a month since—On the night of the 17th we had considerable frost.—The mountains still continue on our right and left, and if any thing more jagged and forbidding in appearance than any we have yet passed. Some of them have the most fantastic forms. Our march for the last two days has been some 35 or 37 miles—I neglected to note a stone we passed on the 16th or rather a hill of stone— all carved up with Indian hieroglyphics—the sun moon & stars—horned frogs—Attempts at the human form divine, were the most frequent forms—they seemed to be of recent date—whether cut in sport or to commemorate some great event we could not tell.

In Arizona As It Is (1877), Hiram C. Hodge describes the petroglyphs at Painted Rocks less telegraphically.

———————————

This mass of rock rises from the surface of the plain to a height of perhaps fifty feet, the uppermost being a broken ledge, from which masses have fallen off, and the whole covering less than an acre of land. On the standing ledge, and on the broken masses at its base, are carved deep in the surface rude representations of men, animals, birds, and reptiles, and of numerous objects real or imaginary, some of which represent checker-boards, some camels and dromedaries, insects, snakes, turtles, etc., etc.; and on the broken rocks at the base of the ledge are found on all sides like sculptured figures, some of which are deeply imbedded in the sand.

At one point, Cochise's tiny band of Apache warriors had a good portion of the standing United States Army engaged in hunting them through the mazelike foothills of the Chiricahua Mountains of southeastern Arizona. The soldiers eventually discovered their main camp, but not before Cochise had made his way elsewhere. Lying near the hamlet of Dragoon, this natural rock fortress overlooks a great expanse of flatland that has served for centuries as a highway from the Apachería to the interior of Mexico. The shipwrecked Alvar Núñez Cabeza de Vaca is believed to have passed nearby on his eight-year walk across the continent from Florida to northern Mexico.

An unsympathetic reporter for the San Francisco Morning Call *describes a visit to the stronghold not long after Cochise's ultimate surrender to the United States Army in 1872. His grudging account at least nods to the Apaches' sophisticated tactical use of the rugged landscape.*

Cochise's stronghold, as this barely accessible spot is called, is situated near the northern end of the Dragoon mountains and extends through this range from the Sulphur Spring valley to that of the San Pedro. It is a craggy break, whose bold and rugged aperture strikes the eye from the summit of the Chiricahua mountains, fifty miles away, and which increases in unevenness and asperity as the traveller approaches it. We had often heard from some of the scouts that a visit to this cañon would amply repay the admirer of wild and weird scenery; but as the trail to the more extreme southern portion of the Territory does not lie through this pass, and as there seemed to be serious doubts as to the possibility of striking water in the stronghold, we should have undoubtedly passed it by, had not a lucky circumstance induced us to change our proposed route. At Camp Bowie we happened to meet Lieutenant Robert Hanna, of the Sixth Cavalry, with a company of Indian scouts, on his way to the Huachuca mountains. As we were wending our way in the same direction, and as there is always a certain sense of security in traveling under the aegis of the stars and stripes, we very gladly accepted the Lieutenant's proffered hospitality, and "for the second time in life enlisted in the line." Lieutenant Hanna being in a hurry—which we find is a peculiarity of United States officers—thought he would take the shortest cut across the Dragoon mountains, and decided upon attempting a passage through Cochise's cañon, water or no water. Every one immediately assented, and was glad even to risk the possibility of a dry camp to be afforded a view of the grandest scenery in southern Arizona. We accordingly broke up camp at daylight, and hurrying across the Sulphur Spring valley, reached the mouth of the cañon at noon. A beautiful grove of live oaks lures you into the more inaccessible portion of the cañon, and if you have faith in maps you will see—on the map—a beautiful spring, which bears the name of Cochise Spring. The dried-up water-hole was there, but, from its geological appearance, we would be willing to assert that the fountain's source had given out long ere the youthful Cochise romped in childish sport on the verdant carpet before us, or practised with his little bow on lizards and pee-wees. Through this beautiful woodland scenery an old Indian trail winds slowly up a gentle acclivity, and taking an abrupt turn, brings you suddenly to the mouth of the cañon, which, owing to the proximity of its sides, and an arched tendency in the rocks above, reminds you forcibly of Dante's dark entrance to the Inferno, and you unwittingly look above for the lines in which an invitation was extended to the visitor to leave all hope behind. One looks appalled at this pass as a strategical position, and cannot help thinking of the reckless bravery that must have characterized our countrymen who dared to track Cochise to his lair, and venture within the range of his rifle.

Every rock is a redoubt, every bowlder a fortress from behind which the murderous Apache could hurl defiantly his primitive means of destruction, as well as the more modern one learned from constant warfare with the whites, and from which at the least wavering sign on the part of the assailant he could at his chieftain's bidding dash out and ply the scalping knife to his heart's content. Layers of ascending rocks, still more precipitous and ragged, form a series of safer retreats in case of need; but we doubt if ever they were used, save against inimical Indians, who may have fought the Apache in his own peculiar mode. A small and narrow passage, barely wide enough for a pack mule, winds its tortuous way through this second stronghold, and finally opens into a sort of basin, surrounded by nobler peaks, which bear a luxuriant vegetation. We found the trail impassible in many places, owing to the fact that it has not been travelled for years, and was consequently obstructed by brush and the projecting limbs of trees; but a passage was soon cut through by our Indian scouts, and we managed to squeeze through at the expense of some of our outer garments, and an occasional refusal to proceed on the part of our mules. In this basin lies the bed of a creek, through which, in ordinary seasons, a lively stream must undoubtedly flow; but owing to the extraordinary drought which has visited the Pacific Coast during the past year, the creek was as dry as the travelers, and with a "same old story" muttered around, we gave our mules a spurring invitation to climb the mountain in front of us. Halting on the other side, we stopped in an immense rocky cavity, from which a beautiful view of the Sulphur Spring valley below us could be had through a sort of lunette about twenty feet wide. The rocks seemed to have been placed by a natural convulsion into an oval frame of the dimensions above given, through which the eye could gaze miles around into the valleys, and from which, undoubtedly, the Apache videttes watched the approach of the Mexican trains on their way to the more northern portion of the Territory. Our command tarried here quite a while, so enchanting was the contrast between the cragginess around us and the smooth undulation of the valley beyond. For a mile or so further the scenery partakes of no peculiar feature until the painted rocks are reached at the southwestern mouth of the cañon, as it opens into the San Pedro valley. The few rays of the setting sun that can penetrate the cañon were just tinging the tops of this peculiar formation, and brought out conspicuously the metallic colors which permeate these rocks in a multitude of crossing and recrossing filons, the whole presenting a picturesqueness seldom to be found among the freaks of nature. At the base of these painted rocks we found water in sufficient quantity to supply the wants of men and beasts, and immediately made the necessary preparations to camp there that night.

OAK CREEK CANYON

Ohio dentist Zane Grey (1872–1939) moved to Arizona in 1907 to take up a new career as a writer. From his magnificent cabin near Kohls Ranch, on the Mogollon Rim near Payson, he proceeded to write scores of Westerns, among them his famous Riders of the Purple Sage *(1912) and* The Code of the West *(1934). Grey's home was a famous Arizona landmark until it was destroyed by the Dude Fire in the summer of 1990.*

In The Call of the Canyon *(1924), from which this passage is taken, a young woman travels west to find her fiancé, who is recuperating from wounds suffered in World War I. She finally tracks him down at the bottom of Oak Creek Canyon in Yavapai County. Glenn Kilbourne refuses to leave his idyllic home, and Carley Burke returns, dejected, to New York, where she considers the pool halls, gutter drunks, flappers, and other horrors and then heads back to Arizona, where she marries Glenn and lives happily ever after.*

"Wal, hyar's Oak Creek Canyon," called the [stagecoach] driver.

Carley, rousing out of her weary preoccupation, opened her eyes to see that the driver had halted at a turn of the road, where apparently it descended a fearful declivity.

The very forest-fringed earth seemed to have opened into a deep abyss, ribbed by red rock walls and choked by steep mats of green timber. The chasm was a V-shaped split and so deep that looking downward sent at once a chill and a shudder over Carley. At that point it appeared narrow and ended in a box. In the other direction, it widened and deepened, and stretched farther on between tremendous walls of red, and split its winding floor of green with glimpses of a gleaming creek, bowlder-strewn and ridged by white rapids. A low mellow roar of rushing waters floated up to Carley's ears. What a wild, lonely, terrible place! Could Glenn possibly live down there in that ragged rent in the earth? It frightened her—the sheer sudden plunge of it from the heights. Far down the gorge a purple light shone on the forested floor. And on the moment the sun burst through the clouds and sent a golden blaze down into the depths, transforming them incalculably. The great cliffs turned gold, the creek changed to glancing silver, the green of trees vividly freshened, and in the clefts rays of sunlight burned into the blue shadows. Carley had never gazed upon a scene like this. Hostile and prejudiced, she yet felt wrung from her an acknowledgment of beauty and grandeur. But wild, violent, savage! Not livable! This insulated rift in the crust of the earth was a gigantic burrow for beasts, perhaps for outlawed men—not for a civilized person—not for Glenn Kilbourne.

"Don't be scart, ma'am," spoke up the driver. "It's safe if you're careful. An' I've druv this manys the time."

Carley's heartbeats thumped at her side, rather denying her taunted assurance of fearlessness. Then the rickety vehicle started down at an angle that forced her to cling to her seat.

Carley, clutching her support, with abated breath and prickling skin, gazed in fascinated suspense over the rim of the gorge. Sometimes the wheels on that side of the vehicle passed within a few inches of the edge. The brakes squeaked, the wheels slid; and she could hear the scrape of the iron-shod hoofs of the horses as they held back stiff legged, obedient to the wary call of the driver.

The first hundred yards of that steep road cut out of the cliff appeared to be the worst. It began to widen, with descents less precipitous. Tips of trees rose level with her gaze, obstructing sight of the blue depths. Then brush appeared on each side of the road. Gradually Carley's strain relaxed, and also the muscular contraction by which she had braced herself in the seat. The horses began to trot again. The wheels rattled. The road wound around abrupt corners, and soon the green and red wall of the opposite side of the canyon loomed close. Low roar of running water rose to Carley's ears. When at length she looked out instead of down she could see nothing but a mass of green foliage crossed by tree trunks and branches of brown and gray. Then the vehicle bowled under dark cool shade, into a tunnel with mossy wet cliff on one side, and close-standing trees on the other.

"Reckon we're all right now, onless we meet somebody comin' up," declared the driver. . . .

The murmur of falling water sounded closer. Presently Carley saw that the road turned at the notch in the canyon, and crossed a clear swift stream. Here were huge mossy bowlders, and red walls covered by lichens, and the air appeared dim and moist, and full of mellow, hollow roar. Beyond this crossing the road descended the west side of the canyon, drawing away and higher from the creek. Huge trees, the like of which Carley had never seen, began to stand majestically up out of the gorge, dwarfing the maples and white-spotted sycamores. The driver called these great trees yellow pines.

At last the road led down from the steep slope to the floor of the canyon. What from far above had appeared only a green timber-choked cleft proved from close relation to be a wide winding valley, up and down, densely forested for the most part, yet having open glades and bisected from wall to wall by the creek. Every quarter of a mile or so the road crossed the stream; and at these fords Carley again held on desperately and gazed out dubiously, for the creek was deep, swift, and full of bowlders. Neither driver nor horses appeared to mind obstacles. Carley was splashed and jolted not inconsiderably. They passed through groves of oak trees, from which the creek manifestly derived its name; and under gleaming walls, cold, wet, gloomy, and silent; and between lines of solemn wide-spreading pines. Carley saw deep, still green pools eddying under a huge massed jumble of cliffs, and stretches of white water, and then, high above the treetops, a wild line of canyon rim, cold against the sky. She felt shut in from the world, lost in an unscalable rut of the earth. Again the sunlight had failed, and the gray gloom of the canyon oppressed her. It struck Carley as singular that she could not help being affected by mere weather, mere heights and depths, mere rock walls and pine trees, and rushing water. For really, what had these to do with her? These were only physical things that she was passing. Nevertheless, although she resisted sensation, she was more and more shot through and through with the wildness and savageness of this canyon.

A sharp turn of the road to the right disclosed a slope down the creek, across which showed orchards and fields, and a cottage nestling at the base of the wall. The ford at this crossing gave Carley more concern than any that had been passed, for there was greater volume and depth of water. One of the horses slipped on the rocks, plunged up and on with great splash. They crossed, however, without more mishap to Carley than further acquaintance with this iciest of waters. From this point the driver turned back along the creek, passed between orchards and fields, and drove along the base of the red wall to come suddenly upon a large rustic house that had been hidden from Carley's sight. It sat almost against the stone cliff, from which poured a white foamy sheet of water. The house was built of slabs with the bark on, and it had a lower and upper porch running all around, at least as far as the cliff. Green growths from the rock wall overhung the upper porch. A column of blue smoke curled lazily upward from a stone chimney. On one of the porch posts hung a sign with rude lettering: "Lolomi Lodge". . . .

[The proprietors] ushered Carley into a big living room and up to a fire of blazing logs, where they helped divest her of the wet wraps. And all the time they talked in the solicitous way natural to women who were kind and unused to many visitors. Then Mrs. Hutter bustled off to make a cup of hot coffee while Flo talked.

"We'll shore give you the nicest room—with a sleeping porch right under the cliff where the water falls. It'll sing you to sleep. Of course you needn't use the bed outdoors until it's warmer. Spring is late here, you know, and we'll have nasty weather yet. You really happened on Oak Creek at its least attractive season. But then it's always—well, just Oak Creek. You'll come to know."

"I dare say I'll remember my first sight of it—and the ride down that cliff road," said Carley, with a wan smile.

"Oh, that's nothing to what you'll see and do," returned Flo, knowingly. "We've had Eastern tenderfeet here before. And never was there a one of them who didn't come to love Arizona."

SOUTH RIM

After ten years as an expatriate in Paris, writer Henry Miller returned to the United States in 1939 and set out for California from his native New York by automobile. The resulting travelog, The Air-Conditioned Nightmare, *is a fine document of culture shock. The prodigal son disapproved of much of what he saw but wept in joy at his first sight of the Grand Canyon, where he spent several days. Here he remarks on nature, art, and human folly.*

Only the night before, as I was taking my customary promenade along the rim of the Canyon, the sight of a funny sheet (Prince Valiant was what caught my eye) lying on the edge of the abyss awakened curious reflections. What can possibly appear more futile, sterile and insignificant in the presence of such a vast and mysterious spectacle as the Grand Canyon than the Sunday comic sheet? There it lay, carelessly tossed aside by an indifferent reader, the least wind ready to lift it aloft and blow it to extinction. Behind this gaudy-colored sheet, requiring for its creation the energies of countless men, the varied resources of Nature, the feeble desires of over-fed children, lay the whole story of the culmination of our Western civilization. Between the funny sheet, a battleship, a dynamo, a radio broadcasting station it is hard for me to make any distinction of value. They are all on the same plane, all manifestations of restless, uncontrolled energy, of impermanency, of death and dissolution. Looking out into the Canyon at the great amphitheatres, the Coliseums, the temples which Nature over an incalculable period of time has carved out of the different orders of rock, I asked myself why indeed could it not have been the work of man, this vast creation? Why is it that in America the great works of art are all Nature's doing?

The Grand Canyon inspires awe, reverence, tranquility, and even terror, depending on the view of its beholder. The French general Ferdinand Foch,

commander in chief of the Allied forces in World War I, was taken to see the
Grand Canyon, where he spent hours gazing into its depths, transfixed.
Finally he turned to his American escort and exclaimed, "What a wonderful
place to drop one's mother-in-law!"

    In "Easter Sunday, 1988, The Grand Canyon, Arizona," poet Ray
Gonzalez offers another contemplation of mortality in the face of an immor-
tal landscape.

Bodies are resurrected
as the whole earth opens
to show how far we must fall
to keep falling,
how deeply we must fear
the savage god
that tears the distance
into red miles of a planet
we will never reach,
the other side of fear
we will never climb because
the trail to the bottom
leads to the tomb of the river
where the earth continues
to eat itself,
feeding upon the river
that devours the river
until bodies rise
in their own space
to float miles across a canyon
that is not a landscape,
but remains of a great prayer
whose chant cut hundreds of miles
of rock into one big tomb
where bodies suddenly
start falling again,
descending to the bottom
of the inner atmospheres
where gravity grabs us

off the rim,
the river rising to meet us
the last thing we ever see.

Etiological myths—stories used to explain the origins of things, such as features of the landscape or how the elephant got its trunk—are common to all the cultures of the world. One of our present etiologies is the geological theory of plate tectonics; for the Havasupai who dwell in the inner gorge of the Grand Canyon, Earl Paya's version of the origin story does the same job. This excerpt explains one feature of the canyon landscape, a Havasupai Scylla and Charybdis. Pedro de Castañeda, a conquistador who passed this way in 1541, grasped at a comparison that would be meaningful to his compatriots when he remarked that such rocks "were bigger than the great tower of Seville!"

[The ancestral mother of the Havasupai] had two boys, who were big and strong like me. They were wandering around hunting or just roaming around, and they discovered this place which is now called Supai. They asked the old woman where they could get some reeds to make arrows. In those days, people used Apache Plume and Ash to make bows and arrows for hunting, but they wanted their arrows to be different, made from the reeds that grow down here. They asked the old lady, but she told them no. "It's bad for you to go down there where those plants are growing. It's okay to make arrows, but use the plants around here. Don't go down there." But they really wished for those plants.

Then she went on and explained to them. "That place is called Wii Ggaaba (Where the rocks come together). It's a bad place to go because it kills people. The rocks go back and forth, coming together and crushing the people who go there. I'd hate to see you two strong boys killed that way."

That place called Wii Ggaaba is Supai. Long ago, in the beginning, the Creator left it that way.

Even though the old woman told them not to go, they decided to go anyway, telling her they were going hunting early the next day. Instead of going hunting, they headed straight for the Canyon. Maybe they went to where we call Topacoba or Hualapai Hilltop or somewhere along up that way. They sat up there watching the rocks go back and forth, as they had seen before.

One of the boys said to the other, "You said you are a fast runner, so you go first. Go down there to where those plants are growing, grab some, and run back as quickly as you can. Do you think you can do it?"

The other one said, "Yes, I can do it, when the rocks open up. I'll run fast, grab some plants and come right back. I can probably make it back up," he said. . . .

The boys were there on the cliff, and one of them said, "We'll both go. Even if we both die, it's okay." But the other one said, "We should cut a piece of log and put it across our shoulders. Then when the rocks go apart we can run down and grab some plants, and come back. When the rocks come together again, the log will keep it open." So they cut the log and went down. The place where they did it is near here. It's called "Wii Gwal Qthyaañe"—you've probably seen it—that's where they say they came down.

They went down into the canyon and got some of that plant. They were on their way back when the canyon started to come together, but it suddenly stopped because of the log across their shoulders. So that's why Havasu Canyon is called Wii Ggaaba, "Where the rocks come together."

Today, whenever anyone tells this story they always think the twins should have used a bigger, longer log, so this place would have been bigger and wider and longer. I myself think that way.

ARTIFICIAL PARADISES

All landscapes harbor magic, especially for children, who, unfettered, spin battlements of rock and mainmasts of saplings. As do writers: Charles Finney, for one, whose Circus of Dr. Lao *(1935) creates a fantastic Arizona populated by chimeras, dragons, and land developers. Alberto Alvaro Ríos is another. In this lyrical passage from his short story "The Secret Lion," Ríos captures the mystery one of Arizona's common artificial landscapes presents to two five-year-olds growing up in Santa Cruz County on the Mexican border.*

One Thursday we were walking along shouting this way, and the railroad, the Southern Pacific, which ran above and along the far side of the arroyo, had dropped a grinding ball down there, which was, we found out later, a cannonball thing used in mining. A bunch of them were put out in a big vat which turned around and crushed the ore. One had been dropped, or thrown—what do caboose men do when they get bored—but it got down there regardless and as we were walking along yelling about one girl or another, a particular Claudia, we found it, one of these things, looked at it, picked it up, and got very excited, and held it and passed it back and forth, and we were saying "Guythisis, this is, geeGuy this . . .": we had this perception about nature then, that nature is imperfect and that round things are perfect: we said "GuyGodthis is perfect, thisthis is perfect, it's round, round and heavy, it'sit's the best thing we'veeverseen. Whatisit?" We didn't know. We just knew it was great. We just, whatever, we played with it, held it some more.

And then we had to decide what to do with it. We knew, because of a lot of things, that if we were going to take this and show it to anybody, this discovery, this best thing, was going to be taken away from us. That's the way it works with little kids, like all the polished quartz, the tons of it we had collected piece by piece over the years. Junior high kids too. If we took it home, my mother, we knew, was going to look at it and say "throw that dirty thing in the, get rid of it." Simple like, like that. "But ma it's the best thing I" "Getridofit." Simple.

So we didn't. Take it home. Instead, we came up with the answer. We dug a hole and buried it. And we marked it secretly. Lots of secret signs. And came back the next week to dig it up and, we didn't know, pass it around some more or something, but we didn't find it. We dug up that whole bank, and we never found it again. We tried.

Sergio and I talked about that ball or whatever it was when we couldn't find it. All we used were small words, neat, good. Kid words. What we were really saying, but didn't know the words, was how much that ball was like that place, that whole arroyo: couldn't tell anybody about it, didn't understand what it was, didn't have a name for it. It just felt good. It was just perfect in the way it was that place, that whole going to that place, that whole junior high school lion. It was just iron-heavy, it had no name, it felt good or not, we couldn't take it home to show our mothers, and once we buried it, it was gone forever.

The ball was gone, like the first reasons we had come to that arroyo years earlier, like the first time we had seen the arroyo, it was gone like everything else that had been taken away. This was not our first lesson. We stopped going to the arroyo after not finding the thing, the same way we had stopped going there years earlier and headed for the mountains. Nature seemed to keep pushing us around one way or another, teaching us the same thing every place we ended up. Nature's gang was tough that way, teaching us stuff.

When we were young we moved away from town, me and my family. Sergio's was already out there. Out in the wilds. Or at least the new place seemed like the wilds since everything looks bigger the smaller a man is. I was five, I guess, and we had moved three miles north of Nogales where we had lived, three miles north of the Mexican border. We looked across the highway in one direction and there was the arroyo; hills stood up in the other direction. Mountains, for a small man.

When the first summer came the very first place we went to was of course the one place we weren't supposed to go, the arroyo. We went down in there and found water running, summer rain water mostly, and we went swimming. But every third or fourth or fifth day, the sewage treatment plant that was, we found out, upstream, would release whatever it was that it released, and we would never know exactly what day that was, and a person really couldn't tell right off by looking at the water, not every time, not so a person could get out in time. So, we went swimming that summer and some days we had a lot of fun. Some days we didn't. We found a thousand ways to explain what happened on those other days, constructing elaborate stories about the neighborhood dogs, and hadn't she, my mother, miscalculated her step before, too? But she knew something was up because we'd come running into the house those days, wanting to take a shower, even—if this can be imagined—in the middle of the day.

That was the first time we stopped going to the arroyo. It taught us to look the other way. We decided, as the second side of summer came, we wanted to go into the mountains. They were still mountains then. We went running in one summer Thursday morning, my friend Sergio and I, into my mother's kitchen, and said, well, what'zin, what'zin those hills over there—we used her word so she'd understand us—and she said nothing-don'tworryaboutit. So we went out, and we weren't dumb, we thought with our eyes to each other, ohhoshe'stryingtokeepsomethingfromus. We knew adult.

We had read the books, after all; we knew about bridges and castles and wildtreacherousraging alligatormouth rivers. We wanted them. So we were going to go out and get them. We went back that morning into that kitchen and we said, "We're going out there, we're going into the hills, we're going away for three days, don't worry." She said, "All right."

"You know," I said to Sergio, "if we're going to go away for three days, well, we ought to at least pack a lunch."

But we were two young boys with no patience for what we thought at the time was mom-stuff: making sa-and-wiches. My mother didn't offer. So we got our little kid knapsacks that my mother had sewn for us, and into them we put the jar of mustard. A loaf of bread. Knivesforksplates, bottles of Coke, a can opener. This was lunch for the two of us. And we were weighed down, humped over to be strong enough to carry this stuff. But we started walking, anyway, into the hills. We were going to eat berries and stuff otherwise. "Goodbye." My mom said that.

After the first hill we were dead. But we walked. My mother could still see us. And we kept walking. We walked until we got to where the sun is straight overhead, noon. That place. Where that is doesn't matter, it's time to eat. The truth is we weren't anywhere close to that place. We just agreed that the sun was overhead and that it was time to eat, and by tilting our heads a little we could make that the truth.

"We really ought to start looking for a place to eat."

"Yeah. Let's look for a good place to eat." We went back and forth saying that for fifteen minutes, making it lunchtime because that's what we always said back and forth before lunchtimes at home. "Yeah, I'm hungry all right." I nodded my head. "Yeah, I'm hungry all right too. I'm hungry." He nodded his head. I nodded my head back. After a good deal more nodding, we were ready, just as we came over a little hill. We hadn't found the mountains yet. This was a little hill.

And on the other side of this hill we found heaven.

It was just what we thought it would be.

Perfect. Heaven was green, like nothing else in Arizona. And it wasn't a cemetery or like that because we had seen cemeteries and they had gravestones and stuff and this didn't. This was perfect, had trees, lots of trees, had birds, like we had never seen before. It was like "The Wizard of Oz," like when they got to Oz and everything was so green, so emerald, they had to wear those glasses, and we ran just like them, laughing, laughing that way we did that moment, and we went running down to this clearing in it all, hitting each other that good way we did.

We got down there, we kept laughing, we kept hitting each other, we unpacked our stuff, and we started acting "rich." We knew all about how to do that, like blowing on our nails, then rubbing them on our chests for the shine. We made our sandwiches, opened our Cokes, got out the rest of the stuff, the salt and pepper shakers. I found this particular hole and I put my Coke right into it, a perfect fit, and I called it my Coke-holder. I got down next to it on my back, because everyone knows that rich people eat lying down, and I got my sandwich in one hand and put my other arm around the Coke in its holder. When I wanted a drink, I lifted my neck a little, put out my lips, and tipped my Coke a little with the crook of my elbow. Ah.

We were there, lying down, eating our sandwiches, laughing, throwing bread at each other and out for the birds. This was heaven. We were laughing and we couldn't believe it. My mother *was* keeping something from us, ah ha, but we had found her out. We even found water over at the side of the clearing to wash our plates with—we had brought plates. Sergio started washing his plates when he was done, and I was being rich with my Coke, and this day in summer was right.

When suddenly these two men came, from around a corner of trees and the tallest grass we had ever seen. They had bags on their backs, leather bags, bags and sticks.

We didn't know what the clubs were, but I learned later, like I learned about the grinding balls. The two men yelled at us. Most specifically, one wanted me to take my Coke out of my Coke-holder so he could sink his golf ball into it.

Something got taken away from us that moment. Heaven. We grew up a little bit, and couldn't go backward. We learned. No one had ever told us about golf. They had told us about heaven. And it went away. We got golf in exchange.

We went back to the arroyo for the rest of that summer, and tried to have fun the best we could. We learned to be ready for finding the grinding ball. We loved it, and when we buried it we knew what would happen. The truth is, we didn't look so hard for it. We were two boys and twelve summers then, and not stupid. Things get taken away.

Few people seem content to leave the land alone, no matter how well intentioned they might be. In his humorous essay "Toward a Boulder Future," novelist Ray Ring writes of landscape change as a product of the so-called New Age, the international headquarters of which now seems to be Sedona.

The vibes have pretty much gotten back to normal in Sedona—as normal, that is, as the vibes ever get in that town—after last month's hoo ha, the Harmonic Convergence.

The convergence, you may recall, was an event of worldwide notoriety. People came together in better neighborhoods around the globe, where they meditated, chanted, thought deep thoughts and sold each other commemorative tee shirts. The idea was to bring on yet another new age. Something like New Age Mark IV.

Sedona had to be a bull's eye for a lot of this converging because of its vortexes, which, simply defined, are places around which heads spin.

Sedona has four, six, eight, even as many as hundreds of these vortexes whirling away in its eerie rock formations, depending on whom you ask, as long as that person is at least hip deep in metaphysics, which is simply defined as the belief in everything all at once, leading to some kind of higher existence, which then becomes your very own personal new age, sort of.

Anyway, something like 10,000 of the truest believers from all over creation swirled into Sedona and around its vortexes, joining forces with the already nicely spinning local metaphysical community, which resides in such new-age centers as the Astrological Heights condo complex.

For several days there was a great deal of being together in a noncompetitive and nonthreatening manner while still trying to remain awake.

Parking was a problem, of course. A couple of pickup loads of litter were dropped and vegetation got trampled around vortexes like Bell Rock, which many pilgrims were hoping would lift off as a spaceship bound for far-off galaxies where there was ample parking for all.

Some pilgrims believed tickets could be bought for passage on the spaceship, and Sedona's metaphysical deejays had to air warnings that the whole thing was a fraud.

Still, there was a real convergence of profits associated with such essential new-age products as commonplace quartz crystals, which, in metaphysical terms, focus energy, or release it, or heal, or bring inner vision, or allow communication with the dead, the undead, gods, Republicans, beings from other planets or parallel dimensions or California, or several or all of these things simultaneously, depending on whom you ask.

Brisk sales were reported by such new-age shops as the Crystal Castle and Eye of the Vortex, which, in its showroom across from the Bayless shopping center, stocks a full line of crystals and related how-to books and videocassettes, fairy jewelry, pyramids, ion generators, singing dolphins on tape, and eight Harmonic Convergence tee shirts in every hue of the rainbow.

On every corner nomad vendors were hawking their own product lines of crystals and convergence wear. Some of the more determined hawked shirts that had crystals sewn right into them.

Convergence guidance was also being sold by an array of consultants who charged $10 an hour on up. And metaphysical real estate agents reported converging interest in vortex-view lots.

Bell Rock never did lift off.

There is another indication of what this latest new age is going to be like, other than the fact that money will be made off of it, and massive geological formations will tend to remain intact. Smaller geologic formations may not.

Simply put, we may be entering the age of circles of rocks.

Lots of circles of rocks.

The pilgrims created them, left them behind, all through the forest around Sedona's vortexes. Big circles and little circles, made of boulders down to tiny stones that had been dragged and rolled and carried and dropped into new-age alignments.

In the center of each circle of rocks is a pile of more rocks. Some circles have rays of rocks emanating from the pile in the center, or circles of rocks within circles of rocks. Some circles are flagged by feathered sticks. Aerial and ground surveys have spotted variation upon variation in the style of how rocks can be circled.

"We had one about 100 feet in diameter," says Bob Gillies, district ranger for Coconino National Forest, where the vortexes, and now the circles of rocks, are located. "We had a lot of them six to eight feet in diameter, rocks about head size. I have no idea how many are out there. They're all over the place, to the point that they're offensive to some people."

The circles of rocks are known by a variety of names, depending again on who you ask. Medicine wheels. Spirit circles. Prayer wheels. They are supposed to focus energy, or release it, or store it, or fine tune it. They hark back to when the American Indians were having their own new age, and were celebrating with what they had on hand, namely rocks.

Whatever their purpose, Sedona's circles of rocks are not at all harmonic to some people, who don't want to have to watch where they step while hiking in the woods. Some people feel the rocks shouldn't have been disturbed from their natural resting places. Some see it as cult activity and feel bad vibes. Ranger Gillies went so far as to tell the *Sedona Red Rock News* that all the rearranged rocks amounted to "littering" and "vandalism."

"You're getting definite modification of the landscape," says Gillies. "I don't know why everyone has to have their own circle of rocks."

The government, which formulates contingency studies on everything from nuclear holocaust to pine-eating bugs, has been caught by surprise by this sudden overabundance of circles of rocks. "We missed that one, boy, I tell you," says Gillies.

The convergers have diverged now. Who knows how far they'll spread this unlikely form of new-age pollution. We may spend the coming years stepping carefully.

WHAT HAS NOT VANISHED

Arizona's natural treasures can be destroyed by only two agents: eons of geological change and humans. In his essay "The Blob Comes to Arizona" and elsewhere, Edward Abbey repeatedly warned of the damage the land sustains at our hands. Richard Shelton raises the same alarm in his poem "Sonora for Sale."

---

this is the land of gods in exile
they are fragile and without pride
they require no worshipers

we come down a white road in the moonlight
dragging our feet like innocents
to find the guilty already arrived
and in possession of everything

we see the stars as they were years ago
but for us it is the future
they warn us too late

we are here we cannot turn back
soon we hold out our hands
full of money
this is the desert
it is all we have left to destroy

"The deserts should never be reclaimed," wrote John Van Dyke at the turn of the century. "They are the breathing-spaces of the west and should be preserved forever." Van Dyke's words, alas, have not been heeded. The effects of the human presence in the Southwestern deserts—for all their seeming fierceness, a fragile and vulnerable series of ecosystems—are no-where better seen than in the Phoenix metropolitan area, although Tucson

and other Arizona cities are doing their level best to match the boomtown.
Ralph Cameron, a Maricopa Indian, offers hope for a better future in his
poem, "My Land, My Water, My Mountains."

When I was young, I saw my land as I grew up.
The rivers were many and without price.
The mountains there had not been touched.
They were beautiful, tall and big and they stood out.
The land I was born on was clean.
The rain washed it and purified it.
You saw it and it was very good.
Now it is not like that.
I see this.
This is my tradition.
A tree half fallen down with its roots showing—I
    feel
I am like that,
    I say we will stand again.
I see many things are left that haven't vanished yet.
The great lakes of the East are still there.
The tall mountains are still there.
The great rivers of the Northwest still exist.
We see this.
The people will walk again, I say.
We will again have the truth.
Our forefathers did this; they took this; they
progressed up until now.
    I say we can do this too.

ACKNOWLEDGMENTS

This book was conceived in an air-conditioned Yuma barroom during the 1989 annual meeting of the Arizona Historical Society. William Kittredge and Annick Smith's collection *The Last Best Place,* celebrating Montana in literature, had just appeared and was beginning, deservedly, to attract attention. After a few glasses of beer in that cool, dark room overlooking irrigated fields, Interstate 8, and what remained of the Colorado River, it seemed to me that my own home, Arizona, merited such a book—but one of finer focus, celebrating place over people, and of more modest extent than the Montana anthology's 1,158 closely set pages.

At the table with me was Dan Shilling, soon to be named executive director of the Arizona Council on the Humanities; historian-in-training Mark Pry; and Bruce Dinges, editor of the *Journal of Arizona History.* I owe thanks to all three for entertaining my notion that day, and especially to Dan and his staff for their enthusiastic support, part of which took the form of a study grant that allowed me a period of time without distraction in which to gather material for the book.

I am also indebted to the Arizona Commission on the Arts for support in secur-ing permission to reprint copyright selections, and to Ron Steffens, Julie Campbell, Mary Sojourner, Jim Harrison, John Hudak, Larry Evers, Tom Miller, Peter Wild, David Laird, Ray Gonzalez, Roberto Bravo, Adelaide Elm, Richard Shelton, and the staffs of the Tucson-Pima Library, the University of Arizona Library, the Northern Arizona University Library, and the Arizona State University Library for help of various kinds. I thank Alan Schroder for his thoughtful editing of the manuscript. Melissa McCormick has aided me with ideas, research, and love throughout the making of this and my other books.

Thanks are due to the following individuals, agencies, and publishers for permission to reprint selections under their copyright: Don Congdon Associates, Inc., for Edward Abbey's *Desert Solitaire* (copyright © 1968 by Edward Abbey); Oxford University Press, for Aldo Leopold's *Sand County Almanac*; the Arizona Historical Society, for material from the papers of Joseph Harrison Pearce (MS 651) and Sue Summers (MS 776); Rita Magdaleno, for "Fall Reunion"; M. H. Salmon, for *Gila Descending*; Hamish Hamilton Ltd and the Administration de l'Oeuvre de Georges Simenon, for George Simenon's *Intimate Memoirs*; Sierra Club Books, for Page Stegner's *Outposts of Eden* (copyright © 1989 by Page Stegner); Ofelia Zepeda, for her translation from the Tohono O'odham; Viking

Penguin, a division of Penguin Books USA, Inc., for Jack Kerouac's *On the Road* (copyright 1955, 1957 by Jack Kerouac, renewed © 1983 by Stella Kerouac, renewed © 1985 by Stella Kerouac and Jan Kerouac), Frank Waters's *Book of the Hopi* (copyright © 1963 by Frank Waters), and Charles McNichols's *Crazy Weather* (copyright 1944 by Charles Longstreth McNichols, renewed 1972 by Charles Longstreth McNichols); The Trustees of Columbia University in the City of New York, for Joseph Wood Krutch's *The Desert Year*; Confluence Press, for Alberto Ríos's *Iguana Killer* and Nancy Mairs's *In All the Rooms of the Yellow House*; the University of New Mexico Press, for Hank Messick's *Desert Sanctuary,* copyright © 1987; the Utah State Historical Society and the *Utah Historical Quarterly,* for Herbert E. Bolton's *Pageant in the Wilderness*; New Directions, for Henry Miller's *Air-Conditioned Nightmare* (copyright 1945, New Directions Publishing Corporation); Richard Elman, for "Cool Lightning Over Tucson"; Loren Grey and Zane Grey, Inc., for Zane Grey's *Call of the Canyon*; Northland Publishing Company, for C. Gregory Crampton's edition of *Sharlot Hall on the Arizona Strip*; Mary TallMountain, for "Phoenix Night-Watch"; *The New Yorker,* for Richard Shelton's "Sonora for Sale" (from *Selected Poems* [University of Pittsburgh Press] copyright 1973 by The New Yorker Magazine, Inc.); Lawrence Ferlinghetti, for "Mule Mountain Dreams"; R. H. Ring, for "Toward a Boulder Future"; Ray Gonzalez, for "Easter Sunday, 1988, the Grand Canyon, Arizona"; the University of California Press, for Ruth Murray Underhill's *Singing for Power* (copyright 1938, 1966 by Ruth Underhill); Macmillan Publishing Company, for William Calvin's *River That Runs Uphill* (copyright 1986 by William Calvin); Mary Banham, for Peter Reyner Banham's *Scenes in America Deserta*; Harper-Collins Publishers for Barbara Kingsolver's *Bean Trees* (copyright 1988 by Barbara Kingsolver); and the American Folklore Society, for Grenville Goodwin's *Myths and Tales of the White Mountain Apache*.

BIBLIOGRAPHY

Abbey, Edward. *Desert Solitaire*. New York: Lippincott, 1968. Reprint. Tucson: University of Arizona Press, 1988.

——. *The Journey Home*. New York: E. P. Dutton, 1977.

Alcock, John. *Sonoran Desert Spring*. Chicago: University of Chicago Press, 1985.

——. *Sonoran Desert Summer*. Tucson: University of Arizona Press, 1990.

Almada, Francisco. *Diccionario de historia, geografía, y biografía sonorenses*. Hermosillo: Estado de Sonora, 1952.

Alvaro Ríos, Alberto. *The Iguana Killer*. Tucson, Ariz., and Lewiston, Idaho: Blue Moon Press and Confluence Press, 1984.

Arizona Good Roads Association. *Illustrated Road Maps and Tour Book*. Prescott: Arizona Good Roads Association, 1913.

Armer, Laura Adams. *Southwest*. New York: Alfred A. Knopf, 1935.

Armstrong, Blair Morton, ed. *Arizona Anthem*. Scottsdale, Ariz.: Mnemosyne Press, 1982.

Austin, Mary. *The Land of Journeys' Ending*. New York: Century Company, 1924. Reprint. Tucson: University of Arizona Press, 1982.

Banham, Reyner. *Scenes in America Deserta*. Layton, Utah: Peregrine Smith, 1982.

Barnes, Will Croft. *Arizona Place Names*. University of Arizona Bulletin. Tucson, 1935. Reprint. Tucson: University of Arizona Press, 1988.

Bartlett, John Russell. *Personal Narrative of Explorations and Incidents in Texas, New Mexico, California, Sonora, and Chihuahua*. New York: D. Appleton & Company, 1854.

Basso, Keith. *Western Apache Language and Culture: Essays in Linguistic Anthropology*. Tucson: University of Arizona Press, 1990.

Bean, Lowell John, and William Harvey Mason, eds. *Diaries and Accounts of the Romero Expeditions in Arizona and California*. Los Angeles: Ward Ritchie Press for the Palm Springs Desert Museum, 1962.

Beers, Henry P. *Spanish and Mexican Records of the American Southwest*. Tucson: University of Arizona Press, 1979.

Bingham, Sam, and Janet Bingham, eds. *Between Sacred Mountains: Navajo Stories and Lessons from the Land*. Tucson: University of Arizona Press, 1984.

Blueeyes, George. "Mountain Chant." In *Between Sacred Mountains: Navajo Stories and Lessons from the Land*, edited by Sam Bingham and Janet Bingham, 18. Tucson: University of Arizona Press, 1984.

Bolton, Herbert E. *Pageant in the Wilderness: The Story of the Escalante Expedition to the Interior Basin, 1776*. Salt Lake City: Utah Historical Society Press, 1950.

———. *Spanish Exploration in the Southwest, 1542–1706*. New York: Charles Scribner's Sons, 1916.

Bourke, John Gregory. *On the Border with Crook*. New York: Charles Scribner's Sons, 1891. Reprint. Lincoln: University of Nebraska Press, 1971.

Bowden, Charles. *Blue Desert*. Tucson: University of Arizona Press, 1986.

———. *Killing the Hidden Waters*. Austin: University of Texas Press, 1977.

Bowers, Janice Emily. *A Sense of Place: The Life and Work of Forrest Shreve*. Tucson: University of Arizona Press, 1988.

Boyer, Mary G., ed. *Arizona in Literature*. Glendale, Calif.: Arthur H. Clark Company, 1934.

Bredahl, A. Carl, Jr. *New Ground: Western American Narrative and the Literary Canon*. Chapel Hill: University of North Carolina Press, 1989.

Brininstool, E. A. *Trail Dust of a Maverick*. New York: Dodd Mead & Company, 1914.

Brown, Charles O. "Arizona: How It Was Made and Who Made It; or the Land That God Forgot." *Arizona Magazine*, March 1917.

Brown, Nellie. "Tharavayew." In *Spirit Mountain: An Anthology of Yuman Story and Song*, edited by Leanne Hinton and Lucille J. Watahomigie, 285–86. Tucson: University of Arizona Press, 1984.

Browne, J. Ross. *Adventures in the Apache Country*. New York: Harper & Brothers, 1869. Reprint. Tucson: University of Arizona Press, 1978.

Cabeza de Vaca, Alvar Nuñez. *Adventures in the Unknown Interior of America*. Translated by Cyclone Covey. Albuquerque: University of New Mexico Press, 1983.

Calvin, Ross. *River of the Sun*. Albuquerque: University of New Mexico Press, 1946.

———. *Sky Determines: An Interpretation of the Southwest*. New York: Macmillan, 1934.

Calvin, William H. *The River That Flows Uphill: A Journey from the Big Bang to the Big Brain*. New York: Macmillan, 1986.

Cameron, Ralph. "My Land, My Water, My Mountains." In *Spirit Mountain: An Anthology of Yuman Story and Song*, edited by Leanne Hinton and Lucille J. Watahomigie, 259–60. Tucson: University of Arizona Press, 1984.

Castañeda, Pedro de. *The Coronado Expedition, 1540–1542*. Translated by George Parker Winship. Washington, D.C.: United States Government Printing Office, 1896.

Castillo, Paula. "How the Mountains Were Created." In *The South Corner of Time: Hopi Navajo Papago Yaqui Tribal Literature,* edited by Larry Evers, 211. Tucson: University of Arizona Press, 1981.

Cather, Willa. *The Song of the Lark.* Boston: Houghton Mifflin, 1915.

Chatwin, Bruce. *The Songlines.* New York: Viking, 1987.

Chronic, Halka. *Roadside Geology of Arizona.* Missoula, Mont.: Mountain States Press, 1982.

Clark, Badger. *Sun and Saddle Leather.* Boston: Chapman & Grimes, 1915.

Collier, Michael. *An Introduction to Grand Canyon Geology.* Grand Canyon, Ariz.: Grand Canyon Natural History Association, 1980.

Cordell, Linda S. *Prehistory of the Southwest.* Orlando, Fla.: Academic Press, 1984.

Corle, Edwin. *The Gila: River of the Southwest.* New York: Holt, Rinehart & Winston, 1951. Reprint. Lincoln: University of Nebraska Press, 1963.

Coues, Elliott. *On the Trail of a Spanish Pioneer: The Diary and Itinerary of Francisco Garcés.* 2 vols. New York: Francis P. Harper, 1900.

Densmore, Frances. *Yuman and Yaqui Music.* Smithsonian Institution, Bureau of American Ethnology, Bulletin 110. Washington, D.C., 1932.

Diccionario Malcriado. Berkeley, Calif.: Editorial Justa, 1980.

Elman, Richard. "Cool Lightning Over Tucson." *The New Yorker,* 25 May 1987.

Escalante, Fr. Silvestre Vélez de. *See* Bolton, Herbert E.

Evers, Larry, ed. *The South Corner of Time: Hopi Navajo Papago Yaqui Tribal Literature.* Tucson: University of Arizona Press, 1981.

Evers, Larry, and Felipe S. Molina. *Yaqui Deer Songs / Maaso Bwikam: A Native American Poetry.* Tucson: University of Arizona Press, 1987.

————. *Yaqui Coyote Songs / Wo'i Bwikam.* Tucson: CHAX Press, 1990.

Fadiman, Clifton, ed. *The Little, Brown Book of Anecdotes.* Boston: Little, Brown and Company, 1985.

Fergusson, Erna. *Our Southwest.* New York: Alfred A. Knopf, 1940.

Ferlinghetti, Lawrence. "Mule Mountain Dreams." In *Arizona Anthem,* edited by Blair Morton Armstrong, 234. Scottsdale, Ariz.: Mnemosyne Press, 1982.

Fink, Augusta. *I-Mary: The Life of Mary Austin.* Tucson: University of Arizona Press, 1983.

Finney, Charles G. *The Circus of Dr. Lao.* New York: Viking Press, 1935.

Fletcher, Colin. *The Man Who Walked Through Time.* New York: Alfred A. Knopf, 1967.

Fontana, Bernard L. *Of Earth and Little Rain: The Papago Indians.* Flagstaff, Ariz.: Northland Press, 1982. Reprint. Tucson: University of Arizona Press, 1989.

Fuller, H. Wallace, ed. *From the Devil's Playground.* Tucson: Arizona Historical Society, 1990.

Garcés, Francisco. *See* Coues, Elliott

Goodwin, Grenville. *Myths and Tales of the White Mountain Apache*. New York: American Folklore Society, 1939.

Grey, Zane. *The Call of the Canyon*. New York: Harper & Brothers, 1924.

Griffin, John S. *A Doctor Comes to California*. San Francisco: California Historical Society, 1943.

Griffith, James S. "The Doggerel Days of Summer." *City Magazine*, July 1989.

———. "La Corua: A Serpent That Haunts the Underground Veins of Water." *City Magazine*, June 1988.

———. *Southern Arizona Folk Arts*. Tucson: University of Arizona Press, 1988.

Hall, Sharlot. *Cactus and Pine*. Boston: Sherman, French & Company, 1911.

———. *Sharlot Hall on the Arizona Strip*. Edited by C. Gregory Crampton. Flagstaff, Ariz.: Northland Press, 1975.

Halpern, Daniel, ed. *On Nature: Nature, Landscape, and Natural History*. San Francisco: North Point Press, 1987.

Halsted, Byron. "A Day at an Arizona Ranch." In *Arizona Memories,* edited by Anne Hodges Morgan and Rennard Strickland, 39–46. Tucson: University of Arizona Press, 1984.

Harjo, Joy, and Stephen Strom. *Secrets from the Center of the World*. Tucson: University of Arizona Press, 1989.

Harrington, Alan. "Juan and Jack." *City Magazine*, May 1987.

Harrison, Jim. *Dalva*. Boston: Houghton Mifflin, 1988.

Hastings, James Rodney, and Raymond M. Turner. *The Changing Mile*. Tucson: University of Arizona Press, 1965.

Heald, Weldon F. *The Chiricahua Mountains*. Tucson: University of Arizona Press, 1967.

Hinton, Leanne, and Lucille J. Watahomigie, eds. *Spirit Mountain: An Anthology of Yuman Story and Song*. Tucson: University of Arizona Press, 1984.

Hinton, Richard. *The Hand-Book to Arizona: Its Resources, History, Towns, Mines, Ruins and Scenery*. San Francisco: Payot, Upham & Company, 1878.

Hodge, H. C. *Arizona As It Is; or, The Coming Country, Compiled from Notes of Travel During the Years 1874, 1875, and 1876* . New York: Hurd and Houghton, 1877.

Hornaday, William T. *Camp-fires on Desert and Lava*. New York: Charles Scribner's Sons, 1908. Reprint. Tucson: University of Arizona Press, 1983.

Karlinsky, Simon, ed. *The Nabokov–Wilson Letters, 1940–1971*. New York: Harper & Row, 1979.

Kerouac, Jack. *On the Road.* New York: Viking Press, 1955.

Kingsolver, Barbara. *The Bean Trees*. New York: Harper & Row, 1988.

Kolb, E. L. *Through the Grand Canyon from Wyoming to Mexico*. New York: Macmillan, 1914. Reprint. Tucson: University of Arizona Press, 1989.

Krutch, Joseph Wood. *The Desert Year*. New York: W. Sloane and Associates, 1952. Reprint. Tucson: University of Arizona Press, 1985.

Lawrence, D. H. *Mornings in Mexico*. London: Martin Secker, 1927. Reprint. New York: Penguin, 1988.

Lee, Katie. *Ten Thousand Goddam Cattle*. Flagstaff, Ariz.: Northland Press, 1976.

Leopold, Aldo. *A Sand County Almanac*. New York: Oxford University Press, 1949.

Limerick, Patricia Nelson. *The Legacy of Conquest: The Unbroken Past of the American West*. New York: W. W. Norton, 1987.

Lloyd, J. William. *Songs of the Desert*. Westfield, N.J.: The Berryhill Company, 1903.

Lowe, Charles. *Arizona's Natural Environment*. Tucson: University of Arizona Press, 1964.

Luckingham, Bradford. *Phoenix: A History*. Tucson: University of Arizona Press, 1989.

Lummis, Charles F. *Letters from the Southwest*. Edited by James W. Byrkit. Tucson: University of Arizona Press, 1989.

———. *Some Strange Corners of Our Country*. New York: The Century Company, 1892. Reprint. Tucson: University of Arizona Press, 1989.

Lyon, Thomas J., ed. *This Incomperable Lande: A Book of American Nature Writing*. Boston: Houghton Mifflin, 1989.

McCarthy, Cormac. *Blood Meridian*. New York: Random House, 1985.

McGee, W. J. "Desert Thirst as Disease." *Interstate Medical Journal* 13 (1906), 279–300.

McGinnies, William G. *Discovering the Desert: The Legacy of the Carnegie Desert Botanical Laboratory*. Tucson: University of Arizona Press, 1981.

MacMahon, James A. *Deserts*. New York: Alfred A. Knopf, 1985.

McNichols, Charles. *Crazy Weather*. New York: Macmillan, 1944. Reprint. Lincoln: University of Nebraska Press, 1967.

Mairs, Nancy. *In All the Rooms of the Yellow House*. Lewiston, Idaho: Blue Moon Press and Confluence Press, 1984.

Major, Mabel, Rebecca W. Smith, and T. M. Pearce. *Southwest Heritage*. Albuquerque: University of New Mexico Press, 1938.

Matthews, Washington. *The Night Chant: A Navaho Ceremony*. New York: American Museum of Natural History, 1902.

Maxwell, Margaret. *A Passion for Freedom: The Life of Sharlot Hall*. Tucson: University of Arizona Press, 1982.

Méndez, Miguel G. *De la vida y del folclore de la frontera*. Tucson: Mexican American Studies and Research Center, 1986.

Messick, Hank. *Desert Sanctuary*. Albuquerque: University of New Mexico Press, 1987.

Miller, Henry. *The Air-Conditioned Nightmare*. New York: New Directions, 1945.

Miller, Joaquín. *Collected Poems*. New York: Putnam, 1918.

Miller, Joseph, ed. *The Arizona Story*. New York: Hastings House, 1952.

Miller, Tom, ed. *Arizona: The Land and the People*. Tucson: University of Arizona Press, 1986.

Molina, Felipe S. "Growing Flower." In *The South Corner of Time: Hopi Navajo Papago Yaqui Tribal Literature,* edited by Larry Evers, 194. Tucson: University of Arizona Press, 1981.

Momaday, N. Scott. *The Names*. New York: Harper & Row, 1976. Reprint. Tucson: University of Arizona Press, 1987.

Mora, Pat. *Chants*. Houston: Arte Público Press, 1984.

Morgan, Anne Hodges, and Rennard Strickland, eds. *Arizona Memories*. Tucson: University of Arizona Press, 1984.

Nabhan, Gary Paul. *The Desert Smells Like Rain*. Berkeley, Calif.: North Point Press, 1982.

———. *Gathering the Desert*. Tucson: University of Arizona Press, 1985.

———. *Saguaro*. Tucson: Southwest Parks and Monuments Association, 1986.

O'Bryan, Aileen. *The Diné: Origin Myths of the Navaho Indians*. Bureau of American Ethnology Bulletin 163. Washington: Smithsonian Institution, 1963.

Ortiz, Alfonso, ed. *Handbook of North American Indians*. Vols. 9 and 10: *Southwest*. Washington, D.C.: Smithsonian Institution, 1979.

Ortiz, Simon J. *A Good Journey*. Berkeley, Calif.: Turtle Island, 1977. Reprint. Tucson: University of Arizona Press, 1984.

Paya, Earl. "Origin Tale." In *Spirit Mountain: An Anthology of Yuman Story and Song*, edited by Leanne Hinton and Lucille J. Watahomigie, 155–61. Tucson: University of Arizona Press, 1984.

Pattie, James Ohio. *Personal Narrative*. Cincinnati: J. H. Wood, 1831. Reprint. Lincoln: University of Nebraska Press, 1984.

Pearce, Joseph Garrison. "Arizona's First Forest Ranger." In *Arizona Memories,* edited by Anne Hodges Morgan and Rennard Strickland, 125–34. Tucson: University of Arizona Press, 1984.

Perkins, Maxwell. *Editor to Author: The Letters of Maxwell E. Perkins*. New York: Charles Scribner's Sons, 1950.

Pfefferkorn, Ignaz. *Sonora: A Description of the Province*. Translated by Theodore E. Treutlein. Albuquerque: University of New Mexico Press, 1949. Reprint. Tucson: University of Arizona Press, 1989.

Phelps, Charles H. "Yuma." *California Illustrated Magazine*, March 1882.

Powell, John Wesley. *Canyons of the Colorado*. New York: Flood and Vincent,

1895. Reprinted as *The Exploration of the Colorado River and Its Canyons.* New York: Penguin Books, 1987.

Powell, Lawrence Clark. *Arizona: A History.* New York: W. W. Norton, 1976. Reprint. Albuquerque: University of New Mexico Press, 1991.

————. *Southwest Classics: The Creative Literature of the Arid Lands; Essays on the Books and Their Writers.* Los Angeles: Ward Ritchie Press, 1974. Reprint. Tucson: University of Arizona Press, 1983.

Priestley, J. B. *Midnight on the Desert.* New York: Harper & Brothers, 1937.

————. "Remembering Arizona." *Arizona Highways,* December 1949.

Pumpelly, Raphael. *Across Asia and America.* London: Hodder, 1862.

Pyne, Stephen J. *Dutton's Point: An Intellectual History of the Grand Canyon.* Grand Canyon: Grand Canyon Natural History Association, 1982.

Quammen, David. *Natural Acts: A Sidelong View of Science and Nature.* New York: Dell Publishing Company, 1985.

Reichard, Gladys. *Navajo Religion: A Study in Symbolism.* New York: Pantheon Books/Bollingen, 1949.

Reisner, Marc. *Cadillac Desert: The American West and Its Disappearing Water.* New York: Viking, 1986.

Rexroth, Kenneth. *An Autobiographical Novel.* Santa Barbara, Calif.: Ross-Erikson, 1978.

Ring, R. H. "Toward a Boulder Future." *New Times,* September 30–October 6, 1987.

Rothenberg, Jerome, ed. *Technicians of the Sacred.* Berkeley and Los Angeles: University of California Press, 1985.

Ruffner, Budge. *All Hell Needs Is Water.* Tucson: University of Arizona Press, 1972.

Salmon, M. H. *Gila Descending: A Southwestern Journey.* San Lorenzo, N.M.: High-Lonesome Books, 1986.

Santamaría, Francisco. *Diccionario de Mejicanismos.* Mexico City: Editorial Porrúa, 1953.

Saxton, Dean, and Lucille Saxton. *O'otham Hoho'ok A'agitha: Legends and Lore of the Papago and Pima Indians.* Tucson: University of Arizona Press, 1973.

Schulteis, Rob. *The Hidden West: Journeys in the American Outback.* New York: Random House, 1982.

Sekaquaptewa, Helen. *Me and Mine: The Life Story of Helen Sekaquaptewa.* As told to Louise Udall. Tucson: University of Arizona Press, 1969.

Shaw, Anna Moore. *Pima Indian Legends.* Tucson: University of Arizona Press, 1968.

Shelton, Richard. *Selected Poems, 1969–1981.* Pittsburgh: University of Pittsburgh Press, 1982.

Simenon, Georges. *Intimate Memoirs.* London: Hamish Hamilton, 1984.

————. *Maigret at the Coroner's.* New York: Harcourt Brace & World, 1952.

Smith, Henry Nash. *Virgin Land: The American West as Symbol and Myth.* Cambridge, Mass.: Harvard University Press, 1950.

Sonnichsen, C. L. *Tucson: The Life and Times of an American City.* Norman: University of Oklahoma Press, 1982.

Spier, Leslie. *Yuman Tribes of the Gila River.* Chicago: University of Chicago Press, 1933.

Stegner, Page. *Outposts of Eden: A Curmudgeon at Large in the American West.* San Francisco: Sierra Club Books, 1989.

Stegner, Wallace. *The American West as Living Space.* Ann Arbor: University of Michigan Press, 1990.

————. *Beyond the Hundredth Meridian: John Wesley Powell and the Second Opening of the West.* Boston: Houghton Mifflin, 1954. Reprint. Lincoln: University of Nebraska Press, 1982.

————. *Mormon Country.* New York: Duell, Pearce, and Sloan, 1942. Reprint. Lincoln: University of Nebraska Press, 1981.

Summers, Sue H. "My Early Life in Florence." In *Arizona Memories,* edited by Anne Hodges Morgan and Rennard Strickland, 67–74. Tucson: University of Arizona Press, 1984.

Summerhayes, Martha. *Vanished Arizona.* Philadelphia: J. B. Lippincott Company, 1908. Reprint. Lincoln: University of Nebraska Press, 1981.

Sykes, Godfrey. *A Westerly Trend.* Tucson: Arizona Pioneers Historical Society, 1944. Reprint. Tucson: University of Arizona Press, 1987.

Trimble, Stephen. *The Sagebrush Ocean: A Natural History of the Great Basin.* Reno: University of Nevada Press, 1989.

Tso, Agnes. "Male Rain," "Female Rain," and "Awakening." In *The South Corner of Time: Hopi Navajo Papago Yaqui Tribal Literature,* edited by Larry Evers, 95. Tucson: University of Arizona Press, 1981.

Underhill, Ruth. *Singing for Power: The Song Magic of the Papago Indians of Southern Arizona.* Berkeley and Los Angeles: University of California Press, 1938.

Vélez de Escalante, Fr. Silvestre. *See* Bolton, Herbert E.

Van Dyke, John C. *The Desert: Further Studies in Natural Appearances.* New York: Charles Scribner's Sons, 1901. Reprint. Tucson: Arizona Historical Society, 1976.

Walker, Henry P., and Don Bufkin. *Historical Atlas of Arizona.* 2d ed. Norman: University of Oklahoma Press, 1986.

Waters, Frank. *Book of the Hopi.* New York: Viking Press, 1963.

————. *The Colorado.* New York: Rinehart, 1946.

Webb, George. *A Pima Remembers.* Tucson: University of Arizona Press, 1959.

Wheeler, Joseph. *Topographical and Geological Surveys.* Washington, D.C.: United States Government Printing Office, 1873.

Wilbur-Cruce, Eva Antonia. *A Beautiful, Cruel Country.* Tucson: University of Arizona Press, 1987.

Wild, Peter "Months of Sorrow and Renewal: John Muir in Arizona, 1905–1906." *Journal of the Southwest* 29 (Spring 1987), 20–40.

————. *Pioneer Conservationists of Western America.* Missoula, Mont.: Mountain States Press, 1979.

Zepeda, Ofelia, ed. *When It Rains: Papago and Pima Poetry.* Tucson: University of Arizona Press, 1982.

AUTHOR INDEX

✦

SUBJECT INDEX

ABOUT THE EDITOR

GREGORY MCNAMEE is the author of *Christ on the Mount of Olives* (Broken Moon Press, 1991), a book of short stories; *The Return of Richard Nixon* (Harbinger House, 1990), a collection of literary and political essays; and *Inconstant History* (Broken Moon Press, 1990), a book of poems. He is also the coeditor, with James Hepworth, of *Resist Much, Obey Little: Some Notes on Edward Abbey* (Harbinger House, 1989), the editor of *Living in Words: Interviews from The Bloomsbury Review, 1981–1988* (Breitenbush Books, 1988), and the translator of Sophokles's tragedy *Philoktetes* (Copper Canyon Press, 1987). He is the book columnist for *Outside* magazine and a regular contributor to several other periodicals, and he works as a writer and editor.